To Mike —
Thank you for the
support.
Whoop Whoop!

Love,
Jason

Purple Bananas

How Prince Saved Me and Other Selections
from the Soundtrack 2 My Life

Jason Webber

First Edition, 2020
ISBN: 978-1-09832-552-7 (print)
ISBN: 978-1-09832-553-4 (ebook)

For Kathleen

PROLOGUE

From: Jason Webber
Sent: Thursday, April 21, 2016 1:01 PM
To: Steiner, Erica (*IC)
Subject: IS PRINCE REALLY DEAD?????

I just tried calling your phone in a panic. Is TMZ SURE that Prince is the one found dead at Paisley Park????

Goddammit, where was TMZ when I fucking needed them? Their crews seemed to know exactly where one of the Kardashians was at any given time but right now I needed answers. I was about to lose my mind—and not just from the usual internal bubbling cauldron of stress, worry, Prozac, caffeine and Xanax that I lived with every day I went to work at Psychopathic Records, home of the Insane Clown Posse.

I needed to know if my best friend was dead. And I needed to know now.

Working in the entertainment business sometimes sucked – don't let anyone tell you otherwise – but it did have one advantage: You got to network with a lot of cool, equally-stressed out people who knew other stressed out people who worked with the most stressed out people on the planet: Celebrities.

It was 1 p.m. No one seemed to know anything except that "someone" had been found dead that morning around 9 a.m. at Paisley Park, better known as Prince's house, in Minneapolis. The cops, coroner, and everyone were all over the scene but there was still nothing concrete. Just speculation. There had been a confirmed report that whoever the dead person was, he or she was found in the elevator by a custodian.

The news was slow as fuck getting out that day. As a former newsroom editor, I can tell you firsthand that while news happens in 24/7 real time, even in this day and age of social media and instant updates, sometimes getting confirmed, fact-checked, go-with-it style news takes a while. All morning my fucking Facebook feed was blowing up with people sharing news stories from all manner of news sources, some reputable, some not, about whether or not Prince - the musician whose art, persona, philosophy, fashion sense, and sexuality had literally shaped me over the years into the 40-year-old man I was now– was dead.

My Facebook friends, at least 60 percent of the 479 or so I had on that day, had sent me messages, texts, or posted shit on my wall, asking what I thought or if I was OK. Around 11 a.m. That morning I had already made my position quite clear with a posting on my wall:

"No. No. No. Fuck you. It's not him it's not him. It's just a security guard or something. It's not him."

I have a potty mouth in real life but I rarely swear on social media posts because I don't want to offend any of my religious friends; not everyone is as uncouth as me and I try to reign in my lesser qualities at times. But it was just a burst of consciousness posting that I HAD to share. Face it, most of us don't need to share the majority of shit we share on social media, but posting can be an addiction for some weird reason so I had to post it. Otherwise I felt like my head was going to explode like one of those guys in "Scanners" and I'd get brains all over the ICP "Mighty Death Pop" mural on the wall behind me.

Erica, who I didn't know well but well enough (I'd gotten TMZ a few exclusive ICP-related stories over the past three years by working with her) still hadn't answered my email two minutes after I'd sent it and I had been refreshing my browser constantly. Click. I could hear my co-worker Rob, professionally known as Jumpsteady, in the next office over talking to a vendor of some sort who was trying to book a booth at the annual Gathering of the Juggalos music festival that was coming up in a few months. Click. Kitty-cornered from my office was the receptionist cubicle where my friend Will sat, answering phones all day and being tasked out to do everything from go get Violent J's sugar free Red Bull to sew costumes for a show. I absently listened to him talk to a customer about their ICP merchandise order. Click. Click. Click. Still nothing from Erica. Fuck!

I went back to CNN's site and the headlines were still not confirmed as to whether or not it was Prince. I tried to stay off Facebook since I knew it was just going to piss me off, plus I was fucking busy. So I really did not need to hear this rumor that Prince was dead. I had work to do, a partner and a 9-month-old daughter to get home to that night, and likely would be texted later by Jane, the aforementioned partner, to stop and get milk or some cases of La Croix water. Lime for me, grapefruit for her.

Suddenly my cell phone vibrated, indicating a text. I grabbed my woefully beat up, memory-bloated iPhone and checked to see who it was. YES! It was Erica. In between calling her on the west coast (she was three hours behind me) and sending her the email, I had shot her a quick text asking "dude wtf is going on with Prince??? Is it him??? Please tell me it's not."

I clicked on her name and there, laid bare was her response. And my worst fear:

"Yeah dude, its him. The coroner just confirmed it. We don't know anything else right now except it is definitely prince. Im sorry I know you were a fan."

My body went slack and I slumped down into my already uncomfortable office chair. I placed my phone face down on my desk, which was cluttered with CDs, contracts that I'd forgotten to file, post office receipts, and various poster prints advertising everything from the Gathering to an upcoming one-off show by Big Hoodoo, one of Psychopathic Records' newly signed artists.

I'd heard those stories about people being so shocked with sudden grief that they just collapse or become stiff. I even witnessed it once when I worked for the mayor of Toledo. I saw my coworker Megan crumble to the floor by her desk when she received a phone call that one of her parents had just passed away. But it had never happened to me until that moment. A few months earlier, when David Bowie—my second favorite artist behind Prince—was pronounced dead, I ran into the bedroom at 2 a.m. and scared the shit out of Jane, waking her up by babbling "Bowie's dead! Bowie's dead! Bowie's dead!" She panicked at first because she thought I was saying "Baby's dead! Baby's dead!" and I was referring to our baby daughter Kathleen—aka Kat—who was asleep in her crib in the next room. Once she realized it was Bowie and not a case of SIDS, she was sad, but more composed. She hugged me sleepily, told me she was sorry for my loss and knew how much Bowie had meant to me. Hell, I even have a portrait of his face from the "Diamond Dogs" album cover tattooed on my upper right arm. No kidding.

I just couldn't move. I think I was even holding my breath, like I was trying to do a stress release, come-back-to-Earth exercise. OK, Jason, deep breath and hold it. Now let it out. Sloooowly. Let all that tension go and all those dark thoughts in your head be expelled with your exhalation.

I eventually breathed out, but it didn't change the reality of what had happened today. Prince, MY Prince and the Prince to millions of others around the world, was dead. Gone. As in no longer alive on this accursed rock in space we call Earth. As in no longer creating music that once changed my life and was still an important part of it.

I reached up on my left side to the shelf that hung on my office wall and fished around for one of the Xanax bars I usually had chilling there. I broke off two sections of the beige capsule, popped them in my mouth, and swallowed them without anything to drink, wincing at the bitter taste as I struggled to move them down my throat with what little saliva I had left. I was a full-blown Xanax addict and even though I always felt a twinge of guilt every time I reached for one of those four-sectioned pills, I didn't feel shit at that moment.

I instinctively refreshed my Facebook page and already scores of friends had posted messages on my wall asking if I was OK and offering condolences. My friend from high school Heather even suggested flatly–and logically–to "Go home." But I couldn't. I had work, I had ... fuck.

I banged my fist lightly on the desk. Tears hadn't yet hit my eyes, compliments of my Prozac and Xanax supplements, which made crying difficult, but I could feel an apple swelling in my throat. I had to get up and move. I'll be damned if I was just going to sit there on Facebook all day, even though that's usually what I did as a distraction from the constant multitasking I had going on every day. I decided I needed to take a walk through the warehouse or some-thing. Just move and try and get my bearings and let the reality of what was unfolding fully hit me.

"Hey, Jason?"

It was Rob, Violent J's brother, calling over from his office. I liked Rob; he busted his ass for the company and I respected the fuck out of him. But why at that moment did he want to talk to me?

"Yeah?" I croaked, my voice hoarse from the tightness in my throat and my dry mouth.

"Did Prince die?"

I don't know why, but him asking me that question at that particular time made me livid. I cracked. I got up out of my chair and started stomping down the short stairway that led to the first floor of the building where the recording studio, warehouse, and video room were located.

"Yes. That's what I hear" I hollered up towards his office door. I felt if I didn't get out of that building at that moment, I was going to fucking deck the first person who got in my path and asked me "What's wrong, J-Webb?" I stormed out the front door, ripped open the driver's side door to my filthy, slightly reliable-but-goddamn-it's-mine 2008 white Kia Rio and leaned back in the seat, staring out the front windshield at the side of the chain link security fence and gate that marked off the rest of the Psychopathic Records property.

I sat there for a minute, still not knowing how I should be feeling. My eyes were still totally dry. I was confused actually. Just a few months earlier I had no problem shedding a few tears when I heard that Bowie had died, and I stayed up until 3 a.m. texting with my friends Eve and Amanda about the loss of our favorite bisexual Martian. In fact, the night Bowie died, I was over at Eve's house having a listening party to his new album *Blackstar*. Then I came home and was absently reading the news on my phone when the news hit. But that was instant grief that felt like getting hit with a sledgehammer or stepping on a nail. I felt Bowie's loss immediately and had little problem dripping a few tears right away when I heard he'd died.

But this was different. I could barely breathe and in the age of social media, 24/7 connectivity I didn't want to read anymore articles or see all the posts on people's Facebook pages who I knew for a fact didn't give much of a damn about Prince, outside of maybe having his greatest hits album.

Then it hit me what I had to do. And I really, really, really did not want to fucking do it.

I pulled my cell phone out of my pocket and dialed the phone number that I knew by heart but hadn't called in almost two years. I put the cell to my ear and waited. One ring. Two. Three. Well, shit, she must be in a meeting or something or...

"Hello?" croaked the familiar but sob-wracked voice of Sofia. I didn't know how I would feel hearing her voice, but its effect became immediately obvious—I fucking exploded into a howling mess of tears. Choking on my own sobs and feeling the hot tears stinging my eyes and spilling down my face, I just blurted out the first thing that sprang from my subconscious.

"Oh, my God! Sofia, I can't believe it! What the fuck?!"

Sofia didn't answer immediately, she just sobbed into the phone. Hearing her cry made me feel, for a moment, like it was 2001 again and we were still living together. As my mind started to sift through snapshots of what used to be, she managed to stammer out an answer in between sobs and heaves.

"This can't be happening," she wailed, which only made my tears flow even faster. "Jason, he was so young. He took care of himself. Why did this happen?"

"I don't know. I don't fucking know," I sobbed, my raw emotions making me forget that we hadn't been a couple in 15 years or even on speaking terms in two years, since I had gone into Asshole Mode when she started going out with her current boyfriend.

"First Bowie, now this. What the fuck is going on?" she asked. And of course, there were no answers about anything yet. Sofia was right. What WAS going on? It just didn't make any goddamn sense. Prince was well-known for living a healthy life. You could tell from his muscle tone that he continued to work out regularly, even though he was in his late 50s.

"I don't know. I just...I'm numb. He just released his best two albums in years!" And he had. *HITnRun Phase 1* and *HITnRun Phase*

2 had both come out in the past year and they were the perfect "shut the fuck up" retort for the average person who regularly said shit like "Prince's old shit was awesome but his new shit is just wack." Both albums were funky, sexy as hell, and filled with cryptic lyrics that 15 years ago I would've been up all night examining like they were some violet riddle. I continued to listen to Sofia on the other end. And then I imagined how much I wish we could have listened to that album together as we used to do way back in the day every time a new Prince album would drop.

I closed my eyes tightly to break the reverie—waxing nostalgic about the good-enough ol' days I'd spent with Sofia years ago always just made me depressed, angry, and resort to looking at her Facebook page to see if she had gotten married to her current boyfriend.

I knew there wasn't much more to say. I had to get back to work, and presumably she did, too, at the insurance company communications department where she worked. I hated getting off the phone, but at that point there wasn't any room left for conversation. We were just hearing each other sniffle.

"I don't know, but text me if you hear any details about what happened," I requested to her pointlessly, knowing I'd be monitoring the news online every few seconds for updates into the cause of Prince's death.

"I will," she responded, her sobs settling slightly and her voice sounding clearer.

"I love you," I said, not believing I had said those words immediately after they left my mouth. Fuck. That was my Achilles heel. I had never lost my habit of telling her I loved her, even though we weren't on the best of terms and she had a fucking boyfriend who she would most likely marry. Right as I started to beat myself up inside though, she answered me back, "I love you, too."

"OK, I'll talk to you later."

"OK. Bye."

I ended the call and leaned back in the driver's seat of my car. Even though my brain was spinning from both Prince's sudden death and sharing a phone call with an estranged ex-lover, I knew I had to get my shit in order and quick. It was still a work day at Psychopathic Records, and I had to get back to my office.

I wiped my eyes and took a quick look at myself in the visor mirror. Jesus. My face was flushed and blotchy and my eyes were glassy and bloodshot. There was no way I would able to pretend I hadn't been crying. I really didn't want to cry in front of my coworkers, though. This was a rap label, after all. And there's no crying in rap music.

I decided to just make a beeline for my office door and shut the door behind me for some privacy. I got out of my car, locked the door, and then headed back into the building … and ran directly into my co-worker Dougie, not exactly the most touchy-feely guy in the world. But surprisingly, he seemed really concerned about my emotional state.

"Ah, shit, you okay, J-Webb? I heard about Prince," he said with genuine condolence in his voice. Not wanting to break down crying again, I just sighed and said in a shaky voice, "Yeah, I'm doing OK. I just … holy fuck, dude. I just can't believe this."

"Yeah, that's stale as fuck, dog. I'm sorry. You gonna be all right?" Genuinely moved by Dougie's totally out of character sympathies, I gave him a quick bro hug.

"Yeah, man, I'll be OK." I moved passed him and went back upstairs into my beige-walled, messy office and closed the door. I slumped into my chair and reached up and grabbed the other pieces of my Xanax bar. I felt the thin capsule with my fingers and popped in my mouth, swallowing it straight down. I quivered a little at the bitter aftertaste, which always seemed to be an apt metaphor for my addiction. I first got hooked on the baron of benzos back in 2008 when I worked for the then-current mayor of Toledo, who was a total rageaholic, and a verbally and emotionally abusive son of a bitch.

After I mercifully got laid off in the spring of '09, I eventually quit the pills by cutting slowly back on my dosage until I was totally off, only needing an occasional half-milligram pill every now and then for the anxiety attacks that plagued me regularly.

But now I was working in the music industry, taking 50 mg of Prozac in the morning and prescribed 4 mg of Xanax (two bars) every day. I frequently took more than the allotted two to stave off the constant knot of stress in my stomach and to temporarily numb the burnout I had felt for almost two years. It wasn't Psychopathic Records fault I'd turned into an anxiety-ridden, future-cancer-patient-from stress; it's the nature of the music industry. Ask anyone who's worked in it for a long time. Seriously. Ask them.

Now having ingested a full bar of Xanax, the disembodied sense of benzo calm washed over me, making me feel both sleepy and blank-minded. I clicked back on Facebook to see what was going on. Predictably, it was nothing but pearl-clutching, obligatory trib-utes like "RIP, Prince. You were a legend." Reading those tributes pissed me off since some of those posts were from former high school classmates who used to snicker at me when I'd walk down the hallways of Kelso High School rocking my bright purple Levi's jeans that I begged my mom to order from the JC Penney catalog. Suddenly everybody was talking about how much they had loved Prince, when chances are the only album they ever owned was that cash-in compilation that Warner Brothers had released a few years back, *The Very Best of Prince*.

I mindlessly scrolled through the news feed for the next hour, not really giving a shit about all the work I had to do. Every web page I clicked on had some kind of shock and awe about the "sudden" and "unexpected" death of Prince. It was status after status of "Prince CANNOT be dead! Please say it ain't so!" to news site after news site reporting everything they knew from Paisley Park. At that point, the cops didn't suspect foul play or anything, so we'd all have to wait for the coroner's report, which pissed me off because I remember the pins and needles effect of waiting for the results of Michael Jackson's autopsy a few years earlier. Tyka Nelson, Prince's somewhat estranged sister and reputedly the inspiration for Prince's classic song about incest "Sister" from the *Dirty Mind* album, was doing the best she could to answer questions and handle everything as it came from all directions. Then the news dropped about how Prince apparently didn't leave a will behind. That did it for me. I couldn't read anymore.

I closed my Google Chrome browser and then went back to my work email inbox, which was about 26,000 messages of Juggalos begging to be signed, to messages from our representative Tyler at RED, a Sony-owned music distribution company that got our product into stores—the few music stores that were left anyway—as well as getting them onto iTunes and the streaming sites, where most of the money in recorded music is made these days.

Trying to busy myself with work, my phone kept buzzing with text messages from friends asking me if I was OK. I was starting to get tired of pasting the sentence "Yeah I'm OK. Just in shock and disbelief" into the text box of every message I received but for once, I kept my brain in check and said to my id "Dude, these people care about you and they know how much Prince meant to you. Accept their condolences with appreciation and just shut the fuck up."

That was the thing—every one of my friends, even the casual ones, knew of my obsession with the Purple One, which began when I was about 15 and had carried for 25 years. My Facebook photos section was positively crammed with evidence of my Prince adoration. There were pictures of me dressed in a crushed velvet overcoat and too-big matching baggy pants, a ruffled, turtlenecked poet shirt like the one Prince wore in "Purple Rain." There was me just last year going to see Prince play his first Detroit concert in 13-years, dressed in full Prince regalia – itchy curly wig and all—with my arm around

Michelle, Violent J's wife. There was me at one of my friend Rude Boy's frequent old school funk dance parties, which mostly focused on Prince and old school funk. That night I had dressed in my Prince costume and did a performance on stage as Prince, singing over his vocals. There was one that was a few years older. I was wearing my 32-inch waisted leather pants and a poet shirt that I'd ordered from a Renaissance/medieval garb online shop and was at Prince Vs. Michael Jackson party at St. Andrew's Hall in Downtown Detroit. I was with a girl named Elaine at the time and I remember we left because the crowd sucked. If you're gonna dance to Prince music, atmosphere is of utmost importance.

There were dozens of other pictures too, going even further back. One of me circa 2011 and about 40 pounds lighter, rocking the aforementioned leathers and a purple, slightly ruffled button up shirt that was more Hendrix than Prince but was still fresh enough to wear to a Prince dance party. And then ... Jesus, I totally forgot about this pic. It was a photo of me from 1997 when I was still living in Longview, Washington, doing Prince karaoke in my high school purple Levi's and a garment I ordered from International Male called "the ultimate poet shirt." Looking back, it's a miracle I didn't get stomped by a homophobic trucker, logger, or mill worker that night while daring to wear that outfit in a good ol' boys, blue collar town like Longview, Washington, which is the same Longview that Green Day wrote a song about on their *Dookie* album. To this day, there's not much to do there but smoke weed and jerk off—though meth has sadly overtaken the town as the people's drug of choice.

All these pictures got me thinking about the fact that the love, respect, and adoration I had towards Prince and his music ran a lot deeper than how most people I had grown up with felt about music. I knew people who were into music, but not like I was into Prince. I looked at Prince as not just an entertainer but almost like a Jiminy Cricket or an imaginary guru. The way I studied his albums forwards and backwards like they were a code to be broken, or the way I tried to walk like him, carry myself like him, and even once, at age 17, spent two hours looking in a mirror trying to bat my eyes like him... these were not the ordinary antics of just any music fan.

Growing up I didn't know anyone else who liked Prince. Not a soul. But all that changed in '99 when I moved to Detroit, which Prince often referred to as his "second hometown" and his Detroit fans as "motor babies," and I found fellow followers of His Royal Badness whose obsession ran almost as deep as mine. In Detroit, I could wear a Prince shirt anywhere in the city and be guaranteed that someone would smile knowingly at me.

There was headline after headline, tribute magazine after tribute magazine, and ongoing gossip regarding the drama over who owned Prince's estate, and rumors about possibly unknown heirs. And then, finally, the cause of death was revealed – Prince had an addiction to opiates from living in constant pain. It was probably penance for decades of doing those gravity and groin defying splits and years of rocking high heels. I wasn't surprised really. Shit, let's see any of us perform like he did for all those years and not need to become a human pharmacy to keep the pain away. Prince had established himself as perhaps the best live performer of his generation, gracing us with the sexiest and most awe-inspiring concerts on record. But it came at a terrible price.

The next weeks were a blur to me. I went and saw "Purple Rain" at the Redford Theater in Southwest Detroit, along with the rest of a sold-out crowd, many of whom, like me, we're dressed in Prince regalia. I got my picture taken with an attractive woman dressed in a Wendy Melvoin costume. I saw many familiar faces that I had seen at various Prince concerts and dance parties over the years.

Detroit was filled with Prince memorial dances and I went to nearly every one, dressed in the increasingly sour-smelling velvet suit, which made me sweat so badly I had to dance with Kleenex in one hand so as to dab the sweat from my forehead and neck. It was a joyous time to dance and celebrate the life of my favorite performer, but it still didn't take away the gnawing sadness I felt about his passing. Months later, I would still get misty eyed every time "Purple Rain" came on the radio. Finally, Jane had enough of my moping and said "Look, I get it. I bawled for weeks after Elliot Smith died. So I get it. But most people mourn the loss of their favorite artist by listening to their music and remembering all the good memories and joy that music brought them. You really need to get over this."

I couldn't exactly argue with her. One, you didn't win an argument with Jane. She was smart as they come, and a tough fighter who could no doubt kick my ass after years of playing roller derby. So I just swallowed my sadness and hoped that the ultimate untrue cliché of time healing all wounds would for once come to fruition.

It didn't.

By now April had turned to November and I was buying the 180-gram vinyl reissues of Prince's old catalog, and every time I put that goddamn needle down on the wax and heard that sizzle as the music prepped for playing, it would just take me back to square one in the grief process. I couldn't understand it myself. When my favorite person in the world, my grandfather, passed in the spring of 2009, I was devastated, but as with all family-related deaths, you eventually find the strength to go on and turn the sobs of grief into laughter of "Do you remember that time Grampa ..." moments. Why couldn't I get over Prince's death? I never even met the guy. Then I realized what I had to do – analyze the ways in which Prince had changed, nurtured, and literally saved my life. I had to retrace my life with Prince and his music to chart how his music had helped turn me from a shy, socially sheltered and stunted, stuttering, scared shitless kid into a shy, socially sheltered and stunted, stuttering scared shitless adult ... who had somehow survived this thing called life.

Shall we begin, Lisa?

I.

 I'm three years old. Living on Goodhope Street in Oak View, California. Jimmy Carter is president. Henry Winkler is considered a sex symbol. "Star Wars" is the most popular movie of all time. Disco rules the airwaves.

And Mom and Dad are hitting each other.

I'm standing in the doorway between the living room and kitchen and crying my eyes out, which they seem to be oblivious to. Years later, I'd see a similar scene—eerily blocked almost the same way—in Prince's movie "Purple Rain." But due to my age, I can't pull Dad off Mom and cry out "Please, Dad, she's HEARD you!" like Prince did. I can only stand there and watch Dad hold my mom's wrists as she tries to slap his face while screaming, "You're not taking him for a walk! You're not taking him for a walk!"

Cut and fade. I can't remember how we got there, but next thing I know I'm with Dad in the backyard of our tiny, two-bedroom house. It's pitch-black outside and I'm sitting across from Dad in a light-weight metal/vinyl '70s lawn chair. Brown and white plaid pattern. I can see Dad's white undershirt glowing in the darkness and can hear him crying, while watching him shake slightly as he sobs. I have no idea what my parents were fighting about.

I am an adoptee obtained by this formerly childless couple via the mercy of Ventura County, California Department of Social Services. My parent's story begins in the shadow of the Vietnam

War sometime in 1967. Mom and Dad met at a USO dance when Dad was in the Navy and stationed in Port Hueneme, California, a few miles outside of Ventura, about 50 miles north of Los Angeles. According to Dad, Mom was underage and had been smuggled into the USO dance by my grandmother, who was apparently trying to help her daughter try to find a man in the most "Here's your one chance, Fancy, don't let me down" kind of way. My grandparents hailed from the sticks of Missouri. I have no idea of their back story, but I think they came west sometime in the Depression years and Grampa found work in the oil fields of the California coast. Gramma was not exactly the model '50s housewife because at least one or two of Mom's three brothers have a different daddy. I never knew this as a kid but always wondered why none of my uncles looked alike.

So Mom is at this USO dance. Meets Dad. I guess at the time Mom was engaged to some other dude, so what she was doing at that USO dance in the first place is beyond me. Maybe Gramma hated whoever Mom was engaged to and was encouraging her to find a more appropriate—or at least mom-approved—fiancé. Dad apparently fit the bill.

By all accounts, they were just friends at first, but then something went wrong with Mom's engagement—probably the fiancé having an issue with Mom being "friends" with Dad—and so the unnamed fiancé dumped Mom. Dad stepped in and the next thing you know, they were eloping to Vegas. I think it may have been one of those wartime romance things—Dad shipped out to Vietnam something like a week after they got married.

Dad fought in Vietnam and got severely hurt after being blown out of a truck. After that, he got sent home with a destroyed back, and a severe case of undiagnosed PTSD. Upon returning home, he made a decision he later regretted the rest of his life: He made my mom drop out of beauty school less than three weeks before she was due to graduate. He was so shell-shocked, he just had to get back to his hometown of Rye, New Hampshire. So there were my folks, living with Dad's parents, Frank and Elizabeth. Elizabeth died of a stroke on February 18, 1975–exactly nine months before I was born–and Dad would later profess to seeing her ghost, telling him everything was going to be "okay." Dad says my grandma Elizabeth, who apparently chain-smoked Pall Malls and was a long-suffering Catholic wife, would have "spoiled you rotten" if she had lived to see me. I've seen exactly one picture of her. She looks like a nice enough lady but Dad used to love to tell the story about how when he was a kid, she caught him playing with matches, and proceeded to burn every one of his fingertips. He used to tell me that story after he would whip me with his belt, as if to say "You think YOU have it bad?"

Apparently, my parents couldn't have kids naturally because Dad shot blanks and something was up with my mom's internal workings. And this was in the Nixon years when infertility options were pretty damned limited.

Enter me, that is after about six years of Mom and Dad waiting to adopt a baby via the Department of Social Services of Ventura County. According to my pathetically vague "case history" provided by the Adoption Services portion of the bureaucracy, my birth mother was of German descent and was confined to a wheelchair due to cerebral palsy. My dad was apparently a Mexican field worker who was believed to have returned to Mexico after knocking my mother up.

After my birth mother had me, I was turned over to foster care for three weeks until I was placed into the waiting, tear-streaked arms of Mom and Dad.

Three years later, I experienced my first cognizant memory of the aforementioned domestic incident. Similar screaming and shoving matches between my parents was a semi-regular part of my childhood.

Accompanying my parents' tendency to fight was their commitment to fundamentalist Christianity. My other earliest memories consist of going to church at the Full Gospel Lighthouse in Oak View,

California, a suburb of Ventura where a lot of oil-working families settled after the Depression, including my grandparents and folks. Dad, who somehow was able to parlay some skills he learned in the military into a career in civil engineering without a college degree, would commute 25 miles to Ventura every day, then return home to small town Oak View at the end of the day.

Oak View was the kind of no-name sleepy town that Republicans dream about—mostly white in a state largely populated by Mexicans. Big enough to support two good sized ma-n-pa grocery stores, small enough for the local pizza restaurant and doughnut shop to be the main social hangouts. It was Norman Rockwell territory all the way.

The good parts of my childhood were great, absolutely fantastic. Being spoiled rotten at Christmas and birthdays. Mom's biscuits and gravy. Dad's perfectly seasoned steaks sizzling on the grill. Constant trips to Disneyland and Six Flags. Camping trips at Lake Casitas. When I wanted something—a toy, a treat, whatever—I usually got it. No questions asked.

But on the flip-side, I was terrified of my parents. Misbehavior often resulted in at minimum a tongue-lashing, and oftentimes, a slap or a spanking. At a very young age, I learned not to talk back, even if it was sticking up for myself on those occasions when Mom and Dad were wrong. Around age 4, I was trying on shoes and when my parents asked me how the shoes felt, I automatically answered "Fine," despite the fact that there was tissue paper stuffed into the front of the shoes and I couldn't wiggle my toes. Dad reached in and pulled out the tissue paper, but I had been willing to accept uncomfortable shoes instead of possibly setting off my parents. They both were emotional nitroglycerin at times, and I learned to tread softly from the very beginning. If they got mad, your entire day was ruined.

In 1979, I began attending the preschool at the Full Gospel Lighthouse in Oak View. I remember being terrified every time Mom or Dad would drop me off and go away. I was scared to death they wouldn't come back and I'd be alone forever. Years later while in therapy, I was diagnosed as having an attachment disorder, most likely caused by being adopted as an infant. A baby knows when it's taken away from its birth mother, and according to many experts, this is a form of trauma. A controversial subject to be sure, but I'm positive my adoption had a lot to do with it. Even though Mom and Dad always came back in the afternoon to pick me up, them dropping me off was a frequently tearful experience.

Preschool was an early lesson in how people can suck. There was a kid named Aaron who would always hog the Big Wheel out on the playground and never let me have a turn. I would complain to Teacher Erica or the head teacher Miss Aggas about it, but nothing was ever done. Aaron was a prick. Probably still is.

At home around this time, I was a pretty well-behaved kid, although Mom and Dad weren't hesitant about spanking. It was drilled into me at a very young age that God expected parents to spank their children when they misbehaved. So, I lived in fear of both God, who according to Dad was "always watching me," and my parents.

With the dawn of the '80s, I entered kindergarten, learning to read and write and being taught "science" from the point of view of the Bible. There was no "and then a meteor hit the Earth and killed all the dinosaurs." Rather, we learned that God created the Earth in six days and that Noah's Ark was an actual scientific fact. My teacher, Ms. Stewart, was a stern woman who didn't take any nonsense or misbehaving and corporal punishment was allowed—nay, encouraged—at my learning institution. Welcome to Ojai Valley Christian School. Abandon hope all ye who enter here.

It was Jesus this, Jesus that at both home and school. There was no escape from the church—it was the literal epicenter of all three of our lives. I made a few friends in my little kid Sunday School class, but not so deep down, I was scared to death. Of everything. Mom and Dad were the ultimate helicopter parents, constantly afraid that I was going to get hurt or worse, turn into a misbehaving, hyper kid like my cousins. While other kids were out skinning their knees and getting into trouble, I was playing quietly on the swing set or monkey bars. But I looked at my supposedly ill-behaved cousins with envy. They were having so much more fun than I was. Years later, I found a quote from Mark Twain that made me smile and think back to those young years: "Be good and you will be lonesome." And I was indeed a lonesome kid.

As the Reagan era got underway, my home life was turned upside down when my parents suddenly adopted my brother. I didn't really know what to think. Adopted at two weeks old, my brother was cute and wrinkly with big pores on his nose. All I knew was that one minute I'm getting all the attention from my parents, the next thing I know I'm suddenly old hat because there's a new baby in the house.

Being adopted is weird in so many ways. Not only do you grow up wondering why you don't look like either of your parents, but you never really stop feeling like an outsider. Mom and Dad showered me with love, devotion, gifts, and everything, but despite it all, there was something that still felt...off. Years later I discovered that this gnawing feeling of disconnection was actually quite common among adoptees. But at the time, all I knew is I had to share a room with my baby brother and all he did was cry.

It was now 1981 and I entered first grade at Ojai Valley Christian School. I had a much friendlier teacher this time, Ms. Curren, who spoke to her students like they were adults, not kids. I appreciated that from her and we often had really profound conversations about extinct animals and nature. I wonder what happened to Ms. Curren— she was really too smart to be teaching at a school where the textbooks taught that the Loch Ness Monster was real and was proof of creationism. No, I'm not making that up; they literally said that.

I wasn't a prodigy or anything, but I was a highly perceptive kid and I was starting to tell that despite my parent's Christian-based upbringing, all was not as it appeared. On one hand, I wanted to be a good Christian and make Mom and Dad happy. I wanted Jesus to be proud of me and welcome me into heaven one day. But Sunday after Sunday in church and day after day in my Christian school began to reveal some truths that weren't exactly pretty.

First, there was the death of Philip Massey. In children's church there was this kid who just couldn't sit still. He was always running around when he was supposed to be sitting, and couldn't even calm down enough to bow his head and pray. He was rambunctious, wild, and generally considered a "problem child." I never befriended the kid, but I kind of admired him. Philip was being forced to go to church, as we all were by our parents, but he seemed to be able to brush off the theology that we were being force fed back then. Today, Philip would almost certainly be diagnosed with ADHD and perhaps a form of autism. But in the early '80s, such conditions were almost unheard of.

Then one day Philip didn't show up for church, which I thought was weird because his parents always made him go. When we got home, Dad showed me a picture in the local newspaper. It was Philip. Dad explained that Philip's father had literally beaten him to death, the result of corporate punishment gone awry. I was stunned and wondered to myself if Dad would ever beat ME to death. He had just started incorporating belts into my spankings. I still remember the first time he beat me with a belt, he said in a menacing voice, "That's what a belt feels like."

Philip's death wasn't even the most sickening part of the whole scenario. The following week, Mr. and Mrs. Van, our church leaders, were up at the front of the auditorium like always, when Mrs. Van said in a perfectly cheerful voice, "Hey, guess what, everybody? Remember Philip? He went to be with Jesus. He died!"

My six-year-old heart practically stopped. What in the hell was going on? This kid just didn't "die," he'd been fucking killed by his own dad. And why was this woman so damned cheerful about it? There was a lot of talk in church that day about how sometimes "God chooses people to come home to heaven." Mr. Van, a mean man with greasy gray hair, also said that same day, "When you're sick and your mommy gives you medicine, that medicine doesn't do that healing. It's God."

I didn't know much about life at the time—I was a smothered, sheltered church mouse who'd been trained to practically fear his own shadow. But something in me changed that day. I realized that I was being lied to by the adult world. There seemed to be something really suspicious about the whole thing. Would God—who supposedly loved me—really take a little kid "home" to heaven? I just didn't get how God "loved" me, and the whole thing about "he gave his only begotten son" struck me as just…cruel. Something wasn't right.

But at the same time, I wanted to believe in God because Mom and Dad wanted me to. They loved it when I would say my prayers at night or tell them about the latest Bible story I'd heard or recite the latest scripture that I'd been told to memorize.

It was around this time that I saw a strange man on the TV one day after school.

I was turning around the channels on our new black cable box and I passed channel 24—MTV. This guy was wearing a bright shiny purple trench coat with studs on the shoulder, big processed hair, and sporting a tiny mustache. At least…I thought he was a man. Was he wearing mascara like Mom did? And what was up with those high heeled boots? All I knew is he looked and sounded cool.

My queries about that man had to take a back seat though, as my family prepared for the arrival of my sister. About a year-and-a-half old, she had been found abandoned in a coffee shop in Seoul and before my parents adopted her, her given name was Jin Ah Tae. The story goes she lived in an orphanage where she slept on the floor with no pillow (although a picture we saw of her depicted her in a crib). I remember missing school to go get my sister from the social worker at the Los Angeles International Airport. When I saw my baby sister, I was mesmerized. She was so tiny, so cute, and so loud. But I also was scared because I knew how I'd been treated when my brother was adopted—I was moved into the background. Now that I had another sibling, and the only sister to boot, I was afraid I'd be even more invisible.

Turned out I was right.

Mom and Dad, now dealing with two little kids in diapers, had to spend most of their waking hours tending to my brother and sister; especially my sister because they imagined she was experiencing severe culture shock going from Korea to America. I was a long way from the perch I'd enjoyed as an only child. I retreated to my bedroom, listening to Michael Jackson's "Thriller" on repeat, playing with my toys, and reading Hardy Boys books. I was lonely, confused, scared, and angry. Not only did I need a friend, I needed a guide. Someone who understood what I was going through and could help sort out the chaos that was swirling in my head.

Little did I know that guide would turn out to be a tiny, androgynous Black man named Prince.

II.

$\mathcal{I}$f you were there and you were the right age, you'll remember the summer of 1984 as being one of the best years ever. The Summer Olympics were being held in my California backyard and I got to see one of the torch runners as well as attend one of the rowing events. At the movies, you had "Ghostbusters," "Gremlins," "Indiana Jones and the Temple of Doom." On the radio, you had everyone from Michael Jackson and Madonna to Bruce Springsteen and about a dozen '80s one-hit-wonders.

And you also had this guy Prince.

"Purple Rain" was both a movie and an album by this weird looking pixie who I recognized as being the man in the purple trench coat I saw on MTV a few years back. He was suddenly everywhere and "Purple Rain" was a full-blown mania. But I was forbidden from partaking in this pop culture phenomenon.

Mom and Dad regularly watched the Trinity Broadcasting Network and listened to everything our pastor Larry Mulkey said from the pulpit at Full Gospel Lighthouse. Both TBN and Mulkey strongly preached against MTV and the godless infidels who populated it. Michael Jackson? According to a televangelist in an ugly brown suit, Jackson was evil because he was a member of the "cult" Jehovah's Witnesses. Boy George? Ugh. Dad about screamed when I ordered a cassette of Colour By Numbers from Columbia House Record and Tape Club. "I like some of their music but I just don't like the way they look," Dad explained, although to his credit, he let me keep the tape.

But he really didn't like the way Prince looked. Here was a man of indeterminable race and sexual orientation who seemed prepared to lead children to Satan via his high heels, like some kind of purple-clad pied piper.

"Is he gay?" Mom asked Dad one night when they were watching a news report on Prince; "20/20" or "60 Minutes" or something.

Dad sneered. "Yes. He's got to be."

I only had a dim idea of what "gay" meant. Sometimes my classmates at Ojai Valley Christian School would describe something—or someone—as gay. I knew it had something to do with boys liking other boys the way you would "like" a girlfriend. It seemed weird to me, but as I watched Prince, I discovered I thought how he dressed was really cool. Yeah, he wore makeup and lace, but it looked awesome. There was nobody else at the time who looked like Prince. And I discovered I actually liked that Prince made some people uncomfortable. It was fun to watch people get agitated because they were getting so offended over something so trivial: A man who dressed a touch effeminate.

The more I watched, though, the more I understood what it was about Prince that made conservative parents so irate. It was the fact that women—particularly young girls—were really attracted to him. My unapologetically racist uncle Jim had an especially strong dislike for Prince, calling him just about every racial slur you could imagine. Uncle Jim also went off when he heard Prince was hanging out with Sheena Easton, who that summer, went from a shy, demure Irish lass who sang James Bond themes and innocuous songs about morning trains to a sultry, vampish sex siren who purred lyrics inviting you to enter her "sugar walls." The word on the suburban street was that Prince was responsible for this new look and attitude from Ms. Easton.

To Christian parents, Prince was a corruptor of the innocent. He made good boys and girls go bad with his invitation to look for the "purple banana" until they took us all away in the white van to the loony bin.

I was strictly forbidden from having anything to do with Prince that summer, but I would listen to his songs on the local rock radio station Q105. I really liked "Let's Go Crazy," an epic guitar rocker that goes down in my personal history as the first song to inspire me to play air guitar. The big hit that summer was "When Doves Cry," a totally bass-free, bittersweet song that stayed at number one on the Billboard charts for five weeks.

The following year, the bluenoses appeared to have won the cultural wars. Prince's song "Darling Nikki" had inspired then-Senator Al Gore's wife Tipper to found the Parents Music Resource Center after Ms. Gore heard her daughter listening to the *Purple Rain* soundtrack. Apparently, lyrics about masturbation and sadomasochism were not suitable for a preteen girl to hear.

I watched some of the PMRC hearings on CNN because Dee Snider from Twisted Sister was part of the panel. I don't remember Mom and Dad watching the hearings, but they certainly had opinions about them.

"All that rock-n-roll you listen to—it's all trash," said Dad one afternoon when he was giving me a lecture about something-or-other. I knew this was one of the grownup world's big lies. Dad liked Elvis and Neil Diamond; did he mean *they* were trash, too? Rock-n-roll was the only thing that really made me feel good. Going to church seemed to make other people feel good, but I never got anything out of it except boredom and guilt. But rock and roll? It gave me a feeling of freedom. I could turn up "Born in the U.S.A." by Bruce Springsteen when it came on the radio and bounce up and down in my room and feel pure elation. The music was my friend.

But the music couldn't save me from Mom's pendulum-like mood swings. On some days, Mom was funny, sweet, and generous, buying us toys or candy at Target. She bought me the View Master edition of Michael Jackson's "Thriller" video, which was awesome. But other days, Mom was irritable, and quick to give you a slap across the face. You never knew what you were going to get. One day, I got smacked and received a bloody mouth because my lips were chapped from the hot California sun. The reason I got belted? I said the word "liar," which was considered a swear word; the preferred word in our house was "storyteller." Other verboten words included "pee," "hate," "kill," and – per Dad's directive – using the pronoun "she" to refer to Mom. Not sure where Dad picked that up but it was probably the military. If I said "She's in the other room," a slap or spanking was likely to follow.

I'll never forget this one time in third grade when Mom had a total Joan Crawford-in-"Mommie Dearest"-breakdown that was so out of control I nearly grabbed a baseball to defend myself. It was summertime and Mom was in one of her moods. The house was a mess, us kids didn't help her enough, etc. After I dutifully cleaned up my room, Mom came into inspect it. She saw a lot of "clutter" on my desk—toys, figurines, and what not. I had straightened it out to where it looked nice, but for some reason, it really set her off.

"Look at this room! It's a pigsty! You call this clean?!" she screamed. The next I knew she was throwing everything off my desk onto the floor. Books. Star Wars action figures. He-Man toys. She even kicked over my "Return of the Jedi" wastebasket by the desk. Her eyes were bulged out and I could see flecks of spit dribbling down the corners of her mouth. I was scared to death and backed away to the other side of the room. I had never seen Mom so upset. My aluminum baseball bat was in the nearby corner and I cowered next to it watching Mom destroy my room like Bob Geldof in "Pink Floyd The Wall." If she came after me, I was prepared to use the bat to defend myself.

When there was nothing else left to throw on the linoleum floor of my bedroom, Mom spun around, panting and completely out of breath. She looked like a snorting bull in a Bugs Bunny cartoon.

"Clean up this mess!" she shouted, thankfully not taking any steps towards me. She stomped out of the room, leaving me and the fruits of her destruction behind her. When she left, I started to cry hot, angry tears. I dutifully picked up the strewn toys and books and put them back on the shelves, but from that moment, something changed. I realized Mom had some kind of deep-seated emotional problem and the only thing I could do was get the hell out of her way when she was like that. Psychology, therapy, counseling, etc. were completely unheard of in our house. Between Dad's then-undiagnosed PTSD and Mom's rages, living in that house was like navigating a mine field.

Thankfully, though, I had music to give me solace.

The following year I was at Gramma and Grampa's house one afternoon when I saw Prince again on MTV. This time he was wearing a suit with clouds all over it and he had straight, pixie-like hair instead of the curls he sported during the *Purple Rain* era. He was singing a song called "Raspberry Beret." At the time I didn't even know what a beret was; I mistakenly thought he meant a barrette, like the cute hair accessories Mom made my sister wear. I loved the video, which had lots of cool animation and Prince sporting heavy eyeshadow and mascara.

And then Gramma walked into the living room.

"Now, who's that?" she asked, a touch of incredulity in her voice, like she couldn't believe what she was seeing.

"It's Prince" I replied, not taking my eyes off the TV.

"Is that a boy or a girl?" Gramma asked without any irony.

"He's a boy," I said, looking over at Gramma, who had gone completely ashen.

"Oh, for heavenly days. What's he dressed like that for?" Gramma asked, concern evident in her voice.

"I don't know. I think it's cool."

Gramma shook her head and started to walk out of the room. "Well, you shouldn't be watching that."

I shrugged. Grownups just didn't get Prince. For that matter, I didn't really "get" him either. I knew better than to ask for one of his tapes, as Mom and Dad would freak out on me, but I dug his music and I dug him.

Prince was my dirty little secret. I would listen to Q105 for hours trying to hear his music and since he was all the rage at that point, the station obliged. They played all the singles from *Purple Rain*, my favorite song being the epic title track, with its "oooo-hooo-hoooo-hooo" scatting towards the end. They also played some of his older songs before *Purple Rain* like "Little Red Corvette" and "1999," which I recognized as the first song I ever heard from the man.

In 1987, my cousin Robbie was staying with us that summer, working as an apprentice for Dad's engineering firm. Robbie, who was approaching 16 years old, was an MTV watcher and since he was so much older than me, Mom and Dad didn't say anything to him when he'd turn on the Top 20 video countdown with Adam Curry. The video to "U Got the Look" was in heavy rotation at the time and I once again found myself enraptured by Prince. Wearing a big fluffy white coat and dangling earrings, Prince steamed up the small screen with Sheena Easton as they bumped and grinded their way through the video.

"Robbie, what do you think of Prince?" I asked one day while we were watching the video for about the third time that day.

"I think he's pretty cool, even if he does dress like a girl," Robbie replied.

"I don't know, I kind of like how he dresses."

Robbie threw me a perplexed look. "You're weird, dude."

I shrugged. "Nah, I just think he's...interesting." Robbie didn't say anything else about Prince after that, instead turning his attention to David Lee Roth's "Yankee Rose" video. The thing I most remember about 1987 was playing "The Legend of Zelda" for hours with Robbie and watching the "U Got the Look" video.

By this time, I was starting to approach junior high, and Mom and Dad were really worried that I was going to turn into a madman once I hit the teen years. Even though I was still only 12, they started wagging their finger at me and telling me not to behave like "a typical teenager." I had no idea what they thought a "typical teenager" did, looked like, or what, but I was terrified of becoming one. I heard horror stories about my cousin's Bubby and Michelle and how at 16 and 17, respectively, they were smokers, both had dropped out of high school, and both treated their parents with "disrespect." I kept my mouth shut most of the time. I didn't want to risk "talking back," which I saw as simply defending my point-of-view, but my folks saw as unchecked rebellion. And since I was becoming a teenager, the fear of "rebellion" was pervasive in our house.

The fact that Dad was again going through a fire and brimstone religious kick didn't help either. We stopped going to the Full Gospel Lighthouse for a minute and went to a Southern Baptist church for a while. Then we went to a Mormon church, which really blew me away. My Dad's business partner and his secretary were both members of the Church of Jesus Christ of Latter-Day Saints, which for some reason royally pissed Mom off. Whenever she'd get pissed at Dad, which averaged at least once a month, she would shout at him shit like "Why don't you go hang out with your Mormon friends!?"

Though we eventually made our way back to the Full Gospel Lighthouse, I resented Dad for church hopping. Here was a man who was struggling with his own spiritual issues and dragging his kids along with him in his own confusion. I was more frustrated than ever.

Thankfully, the summer of 1989 was a magical year for pop culture. The movie theaters were booked with blockbuster hits like "Indiana Jones and the Last Crusade," "Do the Right Thing," and unquestionably the biggest summer movie of the end of the '80s, Tim Burton's "Batman." Being a huge comic book fan, I begged and begged my parents to take us to see "Batman." When they finally did, I raised my eyebrows a little when I saw the opening credit reading

'Songs by Prince'. I'll be damned. I had no idea Prince had anything to do with "Batman."

I loved the movie—at the time it was one of the best movies I'd ever seen—but I was obsessed with the soundtrack. I loved the songs "Trust" and "Partyman" that featured prominently in the film and it was impossible not to flip the cable box dial past MTV, which I was still not technically allowed to watch, and not see the "Batdance" video, featuring Prince dressed up as half-Batman, half-Joker. I used to watch the video over and over whenever Mom and Dad weren't around. It was spooky, funky, and hopelessly catchy.

But despite Mom buying me some Batman movie tie-in T-shirts, including an awesome Joker one that glowed in the dark, Dad refused to buy me the soundtrack.

"I WOULD buy you that *Batman* tape but it's got Prince on it and you know what HE is."

Prince was still not allowed in our house, but that was the least of my problems.

I was in seventh grade at Matilija Junior High School. Life was not good.

I had a moderate to severe stutter that I first detected as early as 10 years old, but by age 13, was in full effect. To my parents, it seemed like my stutter had sprouted up overnight, and they didn't understand why.

"Why are you starting that all of a sudden?" Mom barked at me one day when I was having trouble saying my W's. The truth was my stutter had started to make itself known to me as early as 5th grade. As my stress level increased, so did my stutter. By the time I went from grade school to junior high, I was starting to have stress headaches and what I realize now were panic attacks.

I was picked on mercilessly at Matilija. Most of my friends from grade school suddenly became too cool to hang out with a shy, awkward nerd like me. The kids who *did* want me to hang out with them only wanted me there so they could pick on me. Yet, I was so starved for any kind of social interaction that I actually hung out with these bastards who mocked me at every turn. I remember this red-headed kid named Kevin from my math class. He invited me to go to the skating rink with him on a Friday night. He met up with a bunch of other kids, and when it came time to introduce me, he said "And that's Dork!" Right on cue, about six or seven 13-year-olds all turned to face me and went "Hi, Dork!" I just smiled and weakly waved. The way I saw it, at least I was away from my house.

One night, I had gone to a school dance, running my usual gauntlet of trying to find a girl to dance with me. I timidly asked a few girls to dance in the darkened gym, where during the day I embarrassed myself greatly while trying to do simple exercises. I danced shyly with Kim McCormack, a pretty, sweet girl from my language arts class; I think we danced to "Girl I'm Gonna Miss You" by Milli Vanilli.

As I was feeling pretty well about myself for once, I looked over to the bleachers and I couldn't believe what I saw.

Mom and Dad and my siblings.

What in the ever-loving fuck were they doing there?

Couldn't I enjoy one thing without having my party crashing parents there? What the fuck!?

I stormed over to them, imagining them watching me dance with Kim, probably laughing to themselves.

"What are you doing here?" I demanded, wondering why Mom and Dad were both smiling. "You're not supposed to be here!"

Dad's smile faded.

"Hey, bigmouth! We just came by to say hi. Is that a crime?" Dad asked angrily.

Oh no. I'd pissed him off. I had to try to diffuse the situation before it turned into a major upheaval. But it was too late.

"Yeah, but Dad, I'm just trying to dance and have a good time!" I pleaded.

I don't remember what Dad said after that, but it was obvious I'd killed his buzz. He and Mom really didn't see anything wrong with coming to see me during a school dance. But the fact of the matter is, I didn't want them there. At all. Junior high ran on a totally different set of social rules than elementary school and it was the ultimate in uncoolness if your parents were around all the time.

Mom and Dad got up to leave, grabbing my brother and sister's hands.

"But, Dad, I'm just..."

"We'll talk about it when you get home." They stormed out of the junior high gym.

I regularly felt like I didn't want to go home, but now, knowing my ass was going to be in deep trouble, I was panicked. I ran into the boys' bathroom and burst into tears.

"What's wrong, Webber?" A kid named Joe who I knew from my math class was standing there, looking genuinely concerned.

"Let me ask you something, man," I asked, between sobs. "What would you do if your parents showed up unannounced at one of these dances? Would you be embarrassed?"

"Yeah, probably. Why? Is that what happened to you?" Joe asked.

"Yes. Fuckers showed up and are all watching me dance and now they're all pissed at me because I didn't want them here."

"Shit, that sucks," said Joe. "You gonna be okay, dude?"

I wiped my eyes and sighed. "Yeah. I know I'm going to get it when I get home though. In a perfect world, they'd be the ones being punished." I rubbed my dripping nose on my sleeve. I didn't care if I got snot on it. I was done dancing. Now I had to go home and face Mom and Dad.

When I got home that night, I barged into the living room, ready to defend myself. There was Dad sitting in his recliner. He had a handful of crumpled tissues in his hand and there were tear streaks down his face. I never got used to seeing Dad cry. But I didn't get it. Why was *he* crying?

"Look, I'm sorry, but I just don't think you guys should have been there..."

Dad looked me in the face. "Shut up."

Shit. I knew there was no way I wasn't going to be whipped. He had that glint in his eye and his voice was a low rumble.

For the next half hour or hour—I couldn't tell—I got barraged with Mom and Dad yelling at me how disappointed they were in me, and that they had "every right to be there" and asking me rhetorically, "Do you realize how much you embarrassed your mother and me?"

That was just it—they couldn't understand or comprehend the fact that I was the one who was embarrassed. I was already a social leper, I didn't need my parents there acting like they were coming to a third-grade birthday party ready to dish up ice cream and cake.

The more they spoke the madder I got. They weren't listening to me. They had already made up their minds that I was in the wrong. And at that moment, Prince made his presence known to me.

As I stood there, sobbing, I remembered a line from the song "When Doves Cry." I didn't even have the *Purple Rain* album but I recalled the song from the summer of '84 when it was being played on Q105 seemingly every hour.

The chorus of the song featured Prince pondering why his dad was so brash and why his mother was impossible to please. It just led to empty shouting and fighting and…

I was snapped out of my Prince reverie by Dad jerking me by the arm and shoving me into my bedroom.

"Don't you ever look at me like that!" he bellowed, which confused the hell out of me, because I had no idea I was looking at him any certain way. Jingle-jangle went the belt and snap! The slapping sound of leather meeting flesh filled the room and I screamed. I even screamed when Dad wasn't hitting me. The way I saw it, the louder I screamed, the faster this would be over.

The next thing I remember I'm in bed, crying, and quietly singing "When Doves Cry" to myself.

The next day I had bruises on my ass and legs.

III.

To this day, I still don't know all the details, but all I knew is we had to get out of California and fast. It was just before my 14th birthday and Dad had some kind of business deal go bad that required him to get the hell out of the area. Plus, we were in some kind of trouble with the IRS, too. Mom referred to the IRS as "the people." She'd call him up at work and tell him "We got a letter from the people again."

I didn't know the specifics about what was going on, but whatever it was, it was serious enough to where we had to move out of California without telling anyone. We were headed up north to Longview, Washington, where most of Mom's family was located.

I was not looking forward to starting a new school in the middle of the school year, but I was happy to be leaving Matilija Junior High. That school was just filled with mean people who preyed on those who were different or meek-mannered. I didn't want to stick out, I just wanted to fit in.

In Washington, we moved into a cool, big house out in the boonies. I had a room to myself in the basement while everyone else slept upstairs. Finally, I felt like I had some privacy. My brother and sister were enrolled in a local grade school and I was enrolled in Huntington Junior High School, where I hoped I'd be welcomed and given the chance for a new start.

I wasn't.

If anything, the kids at Huntington were even meaner than the kids at Matilija. Many of the boys – and even some girls – chewed tobacco and it seemed like everyone's dad worked as a lumberjack or at a paper mill. It was quite a culture shock.

Being the new kid in town, I was a prime target for bullies, although I did manage to make one friend—a nice guy named Chris. He lived in a trailer park on my school bus route and I noticed him one day when he had some Dungeons and Dragons books in class. Being a D&D nerd myself, we struck up a friendship. I was happy to have at least one friend.

As I adjusted to life in Washington, I fell in love with the local rock radio station KLYK. The morning drive host was named Darren Day and he was the funniest and coolest guy I'd ever heard on the radio. He played songs like "Time Warp," from "The Rocky Horror Picture Show," which had just been released on video and had become one of my favorite movies. He also played the new songs by Prince, such as the Middle Eastern-influenced banger "Thieves in the Temple," which was apparently from a new Prince movie called "Graffiti Bridge."

The next year, Gramma and Grampa came up for Christmas, which was awesome because I missed them incredibly. We were in Target one day and Gramma took me aside.

"Why don't you go and pick you out some music?" Gramma told me. "That'll be your Christmas present?" I smiled. That sounded like a great gift to me.

I stood in front of Target's then-vast music section and I noticed one album above all the rest—Prince and the New Power Generation's *Diamonds and Pearls*. Gramma said to pick out some music, and, well, Prince was music. But would Mom and Dad get mad?

My grandparents we're the people I could always turn to to buy me forbidden fruit. You know how grandparents are. They're better than parents because 1) They truly do love you unconditionally and 2) They just want to make you happy. As an 11-year old, Gramma and

Grampa had bought me a Madball—the one of the giant bloodshot eye—because I asked for it as a birthday present and they were totally clueless that my parents had forbade Madballs along with Garbage Pail Kids for being "gross." So I got my Madball on my 11th birthday, which was such a delightful "fuck you" since Mom knew she would sound like an idiot if she embarrassed me by putting me on the spot as to why I had asked for something that I knew I was not allowed to have "in my house." Instead, Mom just chuckled and said "That's a grody looking thing!"

I wondered if my folks would have a similar reaction when Gramma and Grampa bought me *Diamonds and Pearls* at Target as my present for Christmas of '91. To their credit, my folks didn't freak out like I thought they would. In fact, Dad told me to bring it with me when I rode with him up to the store. He was pretty poker faced about the fact that his sweet, angel-faced son now officially owned a Prince album, which surprised the hell out of me after years of forbidding me from listening to his music.

So, on that snowy Kelso, Washington day, I got home, slid the *Diamonds and Pearls* tape into my generic Walkman and hit play.

"Thunder..."

The reverb. The multi-tracked vocals. This was fucking awesome. And I had my very own Prince tape in my Walkman. There I sat on my parent's couch listening to a tiny black man in heels singing about sex, Jesus, love, getting stupid while doing a dance called the Jughead, and something about 23 positions in a one-night stand. Hearing my own Prince tape sounded like nothing I had ever heard before, or at least the first time I pogoed on my cousin Brandon's bed to Springsteen's "Born In the USA": The sound of freedom.

Diamonds and Pearls is unjustly recalled as Prince's sellout album because he was debuting his new band the New Power Generation, which included a rapper named Tony M. More than one critic or music writer has pointed out that on *Diamonds and Pearls*, Prince is copying trends instead of creating them, in this case rap and hip-hop. The critics aren't incorrect–Prince was definitely walking in the paved paths of rappers that had come before him. You get the feeling he's trying to follow N.W.A. But truth be told, he comes across more like MC Hammer, Father MC, or Candyman, or any of the other pop rap acts of the day, trying to convince everyone he was comfortable being a mascaraed pixie in a rapper's world.

The thing is, while Prince is probably guilty of being a poseur on *Diamonds and Pearls,* he still pulls off the album nicely, largely due to the urban chops of the N.P.G. bassist Sonny Thompson, whom Prince had grown up with back in Minneapolis. Thompson is a fucking dope bass player, lending his deep grooves to such funky tracks as "Walk Don't Walk," "Gett Off" and of course, "Cream." Yes, let's not forget that *Diamonds and Pearls* is the album that gave us both of those deep blue funky tracks. OK, so the title track is rather maudlin with its "Jingle Bells"-like bridge and corny lyrics. Still, singer Rosie Gaines, adds her amazing background vocals to the track, which elevates an otherwise throwaway song to something of a minor classic. Sadly, *Diamonds and Pearls* would be the only album where Rosie was officially a full-fledged member of the N.P.G. Oh, Rosie, you made the *Diamonds and Pearls* album a dope spot in the Prince canon; let the haters gnash their teeth.

Tony M.'s raps sound jarring today, particularly on the second track "Daddy Pop," but at the time I had the album in my Walkman and on the boom box atop my dresser, it was the dopest thing in the world. And the hologram cover was also cool. I previously had only seen such tricked-out effects on special issues of Dad's National Geographic.

From that moment on it was school, then come home and listen to Prince, a pattern that would be repeated for years to come. Chris didn't get it, he was busy listening to rap and wondered why I was listening to "that fag." To his credit though, he had to admit that "Gett Off" was a jam and the video for "Cream" at least had hot women, so while he jeered me for suddenly becoming a Prince disciple, he was never cruel about it. The rest of my classmates were too absorbed listening to Nirvana – this was 1991 in Washington state let's not forget –and then there's Webber listening to a tiny Black man sing about sex and God: the two things colliding in my head and soul. The rest of the world sat up and spat out their Crystal Pepsi at this dude in assless pants mooning them from MTV.

In those days of Prodigy and Compuserve, we didn't have Wikipedia or the hundreds of Geocities fan pages of the late '90s, so I didn't have a lot of access to do research on Prince, which by this time had hit fever level. I cut pictures out of the issues of Rolling Stone at the school library, looked up old issues of magazines on CD-ROM, including the notorious Prince issue of Rolling Stone released about a year and a half earlier in 1990 in between *Batman* and *Graffiti Bridge*. Written by Neal Karlan, I can still quote passages from that amazing profile today. "...a cross big enough to scare off Nosferatu"..."chewing on Sudafed, nursing a cold"... "though one assumes Prince does in fact sleep." Yeah, I was obsessed with this man.

Every time I would go to the mall I would go to Sam Goody and look at the upcoming release chart for Prince releases. Thankfully, this was back when Prince was putting out something every year; something that I later found out his record label Warner Brothers didn't like because they thought he was oversaturating the market. But to me, and unbeknownst to me, millions of others (I say 'unbeknownst' because I literally did not know a single other Prince fan in the world) there was no such thing - we wanted our Prince fix.

The second Prince album I ever owned was *Graffiti Bridge*. I'd seen the movie a few times on HBO and at the time I thought it was a perfectly good movie about Prince and Morris Day fighting for control over a nightclub. I've since revised my opinion and the film is actually pretty bad. The album, though, is great. The song "New Power Generation" really struck a chord with me, with its call-to-arms lyrics about how the young people of the world want to change things, but they keep colliding with the old folks and their outdated morals and music. It's the perfect raise-your-fist-and-yell anthem for angry 17-year olds.

Other highlights on the album include "The Question of U," "Elephants and Flowers," and perhaps my favorite song "We Can Funk," a duet with George Clinton.

Diamonds and Pearls and *Graffiti Bridge* were the two albums that opened up the Prince floodgates for me. After that, I was hooked. I had to know everything about Prince. His history, the story behind every album, every outfit, everything.

As I waited for the next album to drop, I hit up the cassette rack of Fred Meyer and dug my way through Prince's back catalog. I began saving up my lunch money every day to fund my Prince obsession. Going hungry was a small price to pay for discovering Prince albums that I'd never heard. I started with a cassette that had Prince's third and fourth albums on either side, *Dirty Mind* and *Controversy*, respectfully.

After releasing his first two albums, *For You* and *Prince*, *Dirty Mind* was the first record that Prince made where he showed the world he really was a different kind of artist. His first two albums are solid, late '70s funk and R&B with hits like "Soft and Wet," "Why You Wanna Treat Me So Bad?" and "I Feel for You." But with *Dirty Mind*, Prince shocked the world and made both critics and audiences bolt upright.

Featuring Prince on the cover standing in front of the underside of a mattress, wearing nothing but black bikini briefs, legwarmers, a trenchcoat, and a lascivious sneer, the songs on *Dirty Mind* are fast, raw, and rough—they sound unpolished and almost demo-like. And they're raw in another way, too. Rolling Stone perhaps summed it up best with their five-star review, which gushed "Nothing could have prepared us for the liberating lewdness of *Dirty Mind*."

'Lewd' doesn't even begin to cover this album. The thumping title track kicks things off with Prince begging a woman to get it on with him in his old man's car. The song "Head" is a funky, slinky number about blowjobs, featuring did-he-really-say-that lyrics about Prince getting fellatio from a bride-to-be on her wedding day. He even describes ejaculating on her bridal gown. Naughty, naughty boy, that Prince.

But behind the shocking frankness is the music itself and it's incredible. "When You Were Mine" is my favorite song from the album, featuring a great guitar work out and awesome keyboard playing from Prince's collaborator Dr. Fink.

On the other side of the tape was Prince's fourth album, *Controversy*, originally released in 1981, when I was entering first grade. By this time, Prince was far enough into his career that he was the subject of much gossip and speculation, which was only fueled by the fact he didn't do interviews. He did some in the beginning of his career, but he began to eschew interviews right around the release of *Dirty Mind*. Prince directly addressed the rumors about him on *Controversy*'s title track, rhetorically asking if he's black, white, straight, gay–all questions people wondered about in real life.

What was starting to irritate and confound people about this artist was that he dedicated every album to God and yet he sang songs about incest, threesomes, and blowjobs. How could the same man who recorded "Do Me, Baby?" a lurid bedroom ballad that ends with Prince moaning in orgasm, also devoutly recite the Lord's Prayer on "Controversy?" What were people to make of this sexual revolutionary who recorded the song "Sexuality" as nothing less than a call to arms for his horny soldiers to fuck their way to paradise? People were confused and even scared of this man.

They were even more scared the following year when Prince released the double album *1999*. The release of the album and the accompanying music videos to the title track and "Little Red Corvette" was a major deal to pop culture, because they were among the first videos from a black artist to circulate around MTV.

1999 at the time was THE big Prince album; the one that shot him to the top of the charts and made the world really take notice. It perfected the sex vs. God motif in Prince's work and made the whole world dance. The album opens with Prince's distorted voice reassuring the listener he won't hurt them, he just wants them to have some fun. And *1999* is indeed a fun album that truly defines what became known as "the Minneapolis sound," where drum machines and synthesizers were incorporated in lieu of horn sections. Discovering this album was a lot of fun for me. Songs like "Little Red Corvette," which I recognized as the first Prince song I ever heard, were steeped in synth-drenched sexuality that excited me…and yet Prince sang about God and Judgement Day out of the other corner of his mouth.

Shortly after I added *1999* to my cassette case, I bought the *Purple Rain* album at 13th Avenue Music in Longview and rented the movie from Hollywood Video that same day. That night I watched the VHS down on the basement TV and … holy shit. Like "Saturday Night Fever," I saw my life reflected back to me through the movie. There're definitely some similarities between myself, Tony Manero, and Prince's character of The Kid—all three of us lived with domineering parents that didn't understand us or the respective thing that got us through life. All three of us yearned for a life beyond the walls of our respective neighborhoods. All three of us wanted to escape our mundane, abusive lives. And all three of us had girl problems.

Much like The Kid, I also didn't trust many people. I trusted Chris because he had never betrayed me, but that was it. The scene where Wendy angrily confronts The Kid and accuses him of being a control freak and not giving Wendy and Lisa's music a chance struck a chord with me. So did the scene where The Kid reaches out to his crying mother and goes "Ma?" The scene where Apollonia see's The Kid's parents and goes "Are those your folks?" and The Kid responds, "Yeah. Freakshow." I really identified with that. And like every other horny young man who saw it, the famous Lake Minnetonka purification scene positively warped me. To this day, I still quote the "You have to purify yourself in the waters of Lake Minnetonka" line to any woman I'm with. Sadly, none of them have had the same reaction as Apollonia, who rips off her clothes at the slightest provocation from Prince. Ah, Hollywood, that great manufacturer of make believe.

I saw so much of myself in The Kid, I even took on "Kid" as a nickname in 10th grade. Ms. Kaighan, my typing teacher, obliged when I shyly asked her to call me Kid and I even started writing my assignments as The Kid. This was a relatively short-lived phase as all my friends thought I was crazy and they couldn't take me seriously. But I was just so desperate to be someone other than Jason Webber, he of the lazy eyes and bad stutter. So why not try and be Prince from "Purple Rain?"

Even though my parents didn't get or approve of my fixation with Prince, they still got me the VHS for Christmas that year. Hell, they were probably just tired of me renting the tape from Hollywood Video all the time. I must have watched that movie at least twice a week for six months. To be sure, "Purple Rain" is a product of its time and like most oh-so-'80s movies today, it hasn't aged very well. It's a really sexist film, with both Prince and Morris Day treating women like shit.

Though the movie of "Purple Rain" may be questionable, just about everyone in the Western world probably agrees that *Purple Rain* is an incredible, damn-near-perfect piece of work.

"When Doves Cry" is written as a brokenhearted love song—it's said to have been inspired by Prince's on again/off again girlfriend in the '80s, Susannah Melvoin, Wendy's twin sister. While virginal, 16-year-old me couldn't relate to lyrics about having another person's sweat on your body, other lines from the song where Prince ponders why his mother and father are how they are became mantras to me. On those nights when I would hear my parents raging upstairs, whether at each other or at my brother or sister, I would turn "When Doves Cry" up on my Walkman and try to drown out the noise. Prince clearly understood what it was like to grow up in a house that was like a war zone.

The *Purple Rain* album was a great source of solace during those tumultuous years. I used to silently scream along with the lyrics to "Computer Blue," which really summed up my feelings during those lonely, wallflower days. In the number, Prince screams about how he can't figure out what is wrong with him and why he can't connect with a lover. I hear you, Prince. All my classmates seemed to have girlfriends and boyfriends and then there's me, standing on the sidelines, wishing for something as simple as a hug or kiss.

Of course, the most notorious track on *Purple Rain* would have to be "Darling Nikki," the song that made Tipper Gore clutch her pearls when she overheard her daughter playing it one day. Prince describes a "sex fiend" named Nikki who is reading a magazine and masturbating in a hotel lobby. Not exactly lyrics I could recite during church. This led, of course, to the founding of the Parents Music Resource Center, which got parental advisory stickers labelled on albums with cussing—interestingly enough, *Purple Rain* never received such a sticker.

Around the World In A Day is often considered the first hiccup in Prince's output. From *Dirty Mind* to *Purple Rain*, he could do no wrong. Every album was damn near flawless and filled with all meat and little, if any, filler. But with *Around the World In A Day*, critics and audiences both were blown away … and not in a good way. Released while *Purple Rain* was still selling millions of copies and while the Purple Rain Tour was selling out arenas across America, *Around the World In A Day* couldn't be more different from its predecessor. No more Minneapolis-flavored funk, now it was hippy-dippy psychedelia. Prince was apparently into The Beatles a lot during this time and it shows—almost every critic that's ever written about this album has made a "Sgt. Pepper's" comparison. There's a lot of sitar and chimes on this album and you can practically smell the patchouli. It's a really good album and I love it, even though it's about as far and away from the raw funk of *Purple Rain* as you can get.

Thematically, this album is really important to Prince's career. "Paisley Park," which would later be the name for the big studio complex Prince would build outside of Minneapolis, describes a vision of heaven with girls riding seesaws and everybody happy and grooving together. And of course, *Around the World In a Day* gave us "Raspberry Beret." I don't care if you don't own a single Prince album—chances are you still dig "Raspberry Beret." With the Revolution behind him at full strength, Prince describes working for a racist boss and meeting a girl who took his virginity in Old Man Johnson's barn. It's a great coming of age track and with its sweet, sexy lyrics and hummable melody, "Raspberry Beret" is rightfully considered a classic; at this point, it's basically a pop standard. Other noteworthy songs from the Prince canon are on here as well, such as "America," the album's second single, which flopped, probably because it's a really heavy-handed song for a single. Prince describes nuclear war in a far different way than he described it in "1999." "America" is bouncy and catchy but never quite takes off. Debate still rages to this day if the song is meant to be patriotic or not. While there's every indication that Prince loved his country—witness the rather syrupy ballad "Free" from *1999*—"America" is more of an examination of the problems facing the country, something Prince would revisit to great effect a few years later with the title track from *Sign O The Times*.

"The Ladder," the second to the last song on the album, was the track that had the most personal relevance to me. It's a stirring, lush ballad with Prince singing/talking about a king who is searching for the ladder to heaven. Once again, Prince was singing about the search for salvation in a way that I could understand. There was no preachiness, only passing mentions of God, and yet, the song is devout enough to be sang in any church auditorium. Every night I would pray to Jesus, trying to convince him to show me a sign that he was real and cared about me personally. I read pages from the Bible, but it made little sense—what did books largely consisting of nearly 2,000-year-old gossip and incomplete histories have to do with Jesus dying for my sins?

But here was Prince singing about God's love and the eternal search for inner peace. I'd go to youth group and wish we could sing Prince songs instead of the maudlin hymns they made us sing. "The Ladder" remains one of my all-time favorite songs to this day.

Parade is another classic Prince album, released as the soundtrack to Prince's second movie "Under the Cherry Moon." After the success of the *Purple Rain* album and film, it was unsurprising that Warner Brothers would want Prince to star in another movie. Hell, if Elvis could've been an actor in all those cheeseball movies back in the '60s, why couldn't Prince be a film idol? But "Under the Cherry Moon" totally tanked at the box office and earned Prince jeers from critics. In this film, he played a gigolo in the south of France named Christopher Tracy who's trying to seduce heiress Mary Sharon, played by Kristen Scott-Thomas in her first ever film. With The Time's Jerome Benton as his sidekick Tricky, Prince mugs his way through the movie, basically trying to come off as a cross between Valentino and Astaire.

"Under the Cherry Moon" is technically a bad film, but for Prince fans, it's still an enjoyable one. Prince isn't afraid to be goofy, and his clowning around is pretty infectious. OK, so the guy's not much of an actor beyond playing himself, but what can you do?

But *Parade* makes the "Under the Cherry Moon" part of Prince's career highly memorable. The album has a flavor all its own that sounds like nothing else in the Prince canon. It's very stripped down, jazzy, and quite avant-garde. Consider the album's big hit "Kiss." The whole song is basically Prince's falsetto and a shuffling guitar beat. It's deceptively simple and like "When Doves Cry," contains no bass to speak of. Yet, it works. God, does it work. "Kiss" would become one of Prince's signature songs, but it's far from being the only great song on *Parade*. The opening track "Christopher Tracy's Parade" has a whimsical flair to it, with lyrics about it raining strawberry lemonade. The hypnotic "I Wonder U" is a perfect foreplay song with a slow, sexy rhythm and a lead vocal by the always amazing Wendy Melvoin. *Parade* is interesting because like *Around the World in A Day* and *Purple Rain*, it's attributed to Prince and the Revolution, and you can really hear the full band using all of their individual talents on this album. *Parade* also features what's arguably Prince's most tear-jerking ballad ever, "Sometimes It Snows in April," a forlorn dirge about the death of Prince's character in "Under the Cherry Moon." When Prince died in April of 2016, many fans simply posted the phrase "Sometimes It Snows in April" on their Facebook and Twitter pages. It just said so much about his death. I still get misty eyed on occasion when I hear the track.

I bought the *Sign O the Times* cassette from Music Rack in the Triangle Mall after saving my lunch money for two weeks. The first album since *1999* to be simply attributed to Prince instead of Prince and the Revolution, *Sign O the Times* is a rarity—a double album that contains almost no throwaway tracks. The title track paints a grim reality of America in the Reagan-'80s, referencing AIDS, the Challenger explosion, gang violence, and drug use on the streets. I had never heard things like that covered in a song before. The news wasn't ever really discussed in our house, outside of Dad's blanket statements about how "this country is going to hell." But here was Prince playing CNN reporter.

Years later, the song from the album that would come to mean the most to me was "If I Was Your Girlfriend." This genderfuck love song seriously confused people and still makes shit-kicking, 'Murica-loving men uncomfortable. Prince sings in a digitally-altered falsetto that he dubbed Camille. Lyrically, the song is wonderfully playful with gender. Prince goes so far as imagining and wishing he was a woman so he could understand his mate better. Damn, it's no wonder so many women fantasized about Prince. He really attempted to understand women, which was another reason I idolized the guy so much. I'm not saying he was a saint—there are stories of him making demands on his girlfriends and female proteges to always be immaculately dressed and made up even when they were just doing simple errands. But I do believe Prince genuinely loved and appreciated women and he surrounded himself with tough cookies like Wendy and Lisa. "If I Was Your Girlfriend" stands as a pretty revolutionary song—we need more like it.

Sign O the Times also features the amazing "I Could Never Take the Place of Your Man," which has been covered by everyone from Jordan Knight (sucked) to the Afghan Wigs (rocked). I loved the video, which was taken from the amazing "Sign O the Times" concert movie, which Prince released in theaters instead of going on tour in America. The film is remembered as one of the best concert films ever made, with Siskel and Ebert both giving it a 'thumbs up' review.

"The Cross" is another standout track from *Sign O the Times*. Prince once again puts on his religious robes and sings—or rather shouts—about how Christ is coming back to save the world from itself. Like his other faith-steeped songs such as "The Ladder," "The Cross" spoke to my tormented Christian soul. When Prince sang about God and Jesus, he made them sound approachable and full of love, unlike the fire and brimstone nonsense I heard at the Full Gospel Lighthouse. I like to imagine this song being performed in church auditoriums all over America, though I doubt that's ever happened.

The album ends with one of the best love songs Prince ever recorded, "Adore." Sung in the upper registers of his falsetto and backed by a sexy-sounding saxophone, Prince lays out a seduction attempt of the most epic kind. In 11th grade I copied the lyrics and gave them to the girl I had a massive crush on, Joyce Bremer. I had my friend, Tai, give them to her and while Joyce didn't go out with me, Tai said she loved the gesture. Plagiarism is never acceptable but I knew I couldn't write a love poem better than Prince. Nobody, and I mean nobody, did a love song like Prince. And *Sign O the Times* is a flat-out masterpiece.

I found Prince's *Batman* soundtrack in the cutout bin at Fred Meyer.

Batman contains an awful lot of filler, but there's still a lot to like here. "Electric Chair" is a stomping rock number that Prince performed on "Saturday Night Live." Lyrically, I really latched onto the song because it spoke to my Christian turmoil that continued to dog me during those years. Featuring a chorus about the sins that one commits in their mind (a big theme in my church youth group), this song perfectly summed up the guilt I felt from looking at my female classmates and wishing I could kiss them. "Scandalous" is another great track from *Batman*, a slow, burning, lovemaking anthem with lyrics that advocate skipping foreplay and just getting down and dirty on the floor.

With my education on Prince's musical past complete, I turned to the future and watched the release date calendar in Sam Goody for any future releases. While I waited, I steeped myself deep in my Prince cassettes, almost never leaving the house without my Walkman carrying a tape.

Then one day, there it was—Sam Goody announced that Prince's new album would be dropping that fall! I couldn't wait. I cut class sixth period and ran over to Sam Goody at Three Rivers Mall, and bought the new Prince album, which was titled a mysterious glyph. Call it *the Love Symbol album*, call it, as some music catalogs do, "Androgynous." But when I first saw Prince's 14th album, I called it 'The Trumpet Thing.' His male-female hybrid symbol had suddenly sprouted a new appendage; a horn shaped object with a curlicue tail. It was weird; what did this mean? The first thing that came to mind was that Prince had something urgent to say with this album. Maybe he was about to shout something that he had been wanting to shout for a while.

Indeed, *the Love Symbol album* does start with a shout. On the coarse, raucous opening track "My Name Is Prince," the man literally screams out about how his name is, well, Prince and how he is funky. Well, no, duh. What's remarkable about "My Name Is Prince" is this shouting-style vocal; the first time I heard it, I thought of my mother dismissing the Beastie Boys back in the late '80s: "All they do is yell!" Prince had screamed, yelped, and squealed a number of times in his music but a guttural, throaty shout was something rarely employed. "My Name Is Prince" is a song of angry bravado, the sound of a man who will not be fucked with. Prince, the mascaraed man in heels and lace, sounds as macho as any street rapper in this song. He's loud, aggressive, and dare we say it, pissed off. Here was a trendsetter and icon who had been largely replaced in the public's imagination by rap and hip hop. Now Prince was trying to say "I'm still here, bitches."

Prince's bravado is all over *the Love Symbol album*. The song "Sexy MF," which earned the album a parental advisory sticker, is a jazzy, funky dance number with Prince and Tony M. both rapping about a girl who's a "sexy motherfucker." I always turned down that song when I was listening to it on my Walkman so Mom and Dad couldn't overhear it. "The Max" is another rap-heavy funk song with Prince throwing down how he "goes 2 the Max." Prince's sudden love of rap was kind of surprising considering he had always been some-what anti-rap in the few interviews he had ever done on the subject.

I listened to The Love Symbol album for most of 1992 and on into 1993. I had assembled a pretty good library of Prince's work and I knew my life was going to be purple tinted indefinitely.

But I still had one barrier in my way: My parents.

IV.

$\mathcal{S}$ometimes your folks are just in the mood to bust heads. You can be sitting there, minding your own business, and suddenly they'll come in the room with something like "Hey, do you remember what you said three weeks ago? Yeah, you're in trouble about that." Today, almost 30 years later, I can't remember what set Dad off this one Friday night after he and my Mom came back from hanging out at this tiki lounge they used to go to. All I know is I'm sitting there trying to watch "Prince and the Revolution – Live in '85" and Dad comes in, all pissed off about … something.

I remember protesting because whatever he was angry about was bullshit; it had something to do with my "attitude," which was usually code for "You're not acting happy enough." Never mind that I was an undiagnosed depressive with borderline personality disorder, in our house, "attitude" was everything.

So there's my old man bellowing about my "attitude" and this time he used a prop to illustrate his point. Looking exactly like a fire and brimstone preacher, he snatched the Hollywood Video copy of "Purple Rain" off the table next to the TV and starting waving it like a fucking Bible.

"I know what's causing your attitude problem...THIS!"

And I laughed. Oh, how I laughed. I was crying but I started to laugh my fucking head off. What kind of 1950s sitcom had I found myself in? Dad literally sounded like one of those old fuddy duddies you saw in old newsreel footage and '50s educational films, smashing a record while hollering "Rock-n-roll has got to go!"

How could this be happening? It was 1992 and my old man was sounding like John Lithgow in "Footloose." I can't remember much more about that night. I just remember Dad yanking me out of his recliner and smacking me across the face. I stopped laughing. The next thing I can remember is lying on my bed sobbing.

I knew parents were supposed to hate their kids' music. It was a longstanding tradition that probably went back centuries. I didn't expect my parents to understand my love of Prince. But little did they know that Prince was literally saving my life during those difficult teenage years. It wasn't easy growing up in a house where saying "damn" could get you grounded. Not that it really mattered. I was 16 years old. No car. A small handful of friends who also hated Prince. No girlfriend. No nothing. Just my Prince albums and videos to see me through.

But here was Prince telling me that God loved me. The kind of God who also didn't think sex was dirty. At the same time, I had every asshole preacher in an ugly brown suit telling me that sex was sinful. Prince presented an alternative viewpoint, a total counterbalance to the bullshit I was being fed by my parents. And I knew it was bullshit—their image of a vengeful, Puritanical god who would one day send people like Prince to hell for wearing high heels, makeup, and lace, just didn't make any sense. I couldn't wrap my arms around their idea of God and morality, but I had to pose like I was buying into it. After all, if I acted like the sweet little boy they adopted, I would get my allowance. And then I could take that allowance and buy Prince tapes.

I could hear Prince calling me to arms in the revolutionary song "Sexuality" from the *Controversy* album. Prince's salvation-through-sex message is at its most blatant on this truly fascinating song. He attacks the prudes of the world by spitting lyrics about them being a bunch of "drags" and how the world needs a new type of leader who can organize and unite the sexually liberated of the world into one grinding-and-thrusting horny army. According to Prince, sex can save the world. It's nothing dirty, sinful, or to be ashamed about, which certainly stood in contrast to what I got from my parents or my Sunday school teachers.

I can't even begin to express how much songs like that meant to me at that confused age. A man was singing about sex and God in the same stanza and it didn't seem blasphemous or dirty. It seemed ... liberating. This collision between the sacred and the profane exactly mirrored what I felt going on within me. By Prince singing about it, I was allowed to express the confusion I felt. I wanted to be a good Christian, but I was also a total horndog, just like Prince.

On the "Prince and the Revolution–LIVE" concert there's a part where Prince pantomimes a conversation with God, who is represented onstage by a spotlight and a series of cacophonous piano notes. Prince cries out in anguish "I'm so confused!" Watching it today, it seems kind of hokey, but when I was a teenager, it was no joke. I was confused, too. At another point, he says to God, "I know I said I'd be good but people dig me when I'm bad." God responds with a thunderous roar of piano. That's how I felt. I was so fucking tired of being forced by my family to be "good." And with his music, Prince was basically saying, "It's OK to be bad. God is going to love you anyway."

The way I saw it, Prince's idea of God was of a loving being who created sex as a gift to humanity. Prince never saw sex as sinful or something to be ashamed of. Well, except for the song "Sister" from *Dirty Mind*, where he sings about being underage and his much older sister forcing him to have sex with her or he'd be thrown out onto the streets. That song gave me pause...and I was obsessed with it. On "Sister," Prince is singing about how he is being exploited by his older family member, albeit in a lurid way; I mean, come on, you sure as fuck didn't hear Billy Ocean singing about this shit. I got what Prince was singing about with this short, fast, taunt burst of a song that barely lasts two minutes. Its punk rock urgency lays down a bedrock of anger that Prince channels as he describes being 16 years old and seduced by his 32-year old sibling. Basically, Prince's sister is using him as a sex slave, telling him to do what he's told or he'll be out on the streets. Like Prince's character in "Sister," I was only 16 years old when I first heard that song, and it showed another side of sex that existed in the world—a sinister, dark side that most mainstream folks didn't want to acknowledge. Despite the fact that we live in a world where there are other songs about incest - "Janie's Got A Gun" by Aerosmith, "The Drowners" by Suede, "Fiddle About" by The Who—Prince's "Sister" is in a class of its own, shining a bright light on sexual exploitation that remains shocking to this day.

The thing about Prince's sex songs—and there are hundreds—is that there's usually a celebratory feeling to the songs. And this excited me. It didn't make me want to go out and have sex; I was 16 years old and had only ever kissed two girls, so the thought of actually getting laid was all but impossible. But it did make me realize that the parents, pastors, teachers, and most every other authoritative figure who tried to tell me how to think and act was full of shit. Sex was glorious. It was something to be praised. And oh, how those sex songs helped me during those painful, awkward years of adolescence.

During my senior year in high school, Prince's collision between God and sex really took center stage in my life. I will never forget the time "Little Red Corvette," that great make out anthem of the '80s, got me through my Christian guilt the first time I ever made out—REALLY made out—with a girl.

Her name was Sarah. She was a Swedish foreign exchange student, and don't ask me how, but she seemed to go for me. She was beautiful, with chestnut brown hair, a voluptuous body, and the cutest, sexiest European accent this side of a Bond girl. I sat next to her in Ms. Cooper's English class and despite having zero game with girls, I ended up going out with her … as much as a 16-year-old with no car can really "go out."

But there was a momentous occasion that occurred with Sarah. We were at the skating rink on a Saturday night double date with Sarah's host sister, Stephanie, and her boyfriend Matt, who we all called Boner; I never did find out how he got that name and I'm not sure I wanted to know. After about two hours of clumsily skating and trying not to fall on the hard, flat rink, we two couples left the building and went around to the back.

Sarah and I started making out in that awkward way that all inexperienced 16-year-olds do. My heart was pounding like a bass drum as we tried to ignore the fact that neither of us really knew how to kiss. I was packing a noticeable erection in my jeans and Sarah, who was wearing black stirrup stretch pants kept grinding her hips on mine. I slid my hand up Sarah's sweater to cup her left breast. It was soft, firm … and I couldn't believe I was actually holding a girl's breast.

"D-d-do you mind?" I stammered in a whisper.

My hand on her boob seemed to make Sarah's hips buck against me even harder.

"No, I like it," she said. I kissed her harder and deeper, saliva collecting at the corner of both of our mouths.

But leave it to a religious upbringing to throw a wrench into what should have been the most enjoyable milestone of my lonely teenage life. As I gently squeezed Sarah's breast, feeling the outline of her hard nipple beneath her sweater, the cockblocking angel of Christian guilt suddenly started whispering into my ear.

"You are committing a sexual sin, Jason. This is lust. You're giving into base desires that should be left unexplored."

I tried to block out the inner voice by sliding my hand down Sarah's body and cupping my hand over her crotch, feeling the outline of her panties underneath. And it may have just been my hormone-engorged imagination but I thought I detected the faint feeling of dampness between her legs. This sent my horniness level up a big notch, and as I opened and closed my palm over her crotch, the unmistakable inner voice of Christianity continued to sabotage me.

"This is wrong. Can you imagine what your parents would think if they saw you right now? Can you imagine what Jesus is thinking? He's watching you, you know. He knows exactly what you're doing. You need to stop this. Now."

And then my conscious fought back from a source I didn't expect. Prince.

I suddenly had part of the refrain from "Little Red Corvette" going through my head, colliding against my Christian-stained conscience. I heard Prince's voice singing about how it was Saturday night and that made everything alright.

Hearing the strains of "Little Red Corvette" playing in the stereo of my mind was shutting the door on the Christian guilt. I wasn't doing anything...bad. I was indulging in an ordinary part of life. Here we were. Two consenting teens indulging in the time-honored tradition of heavy petting. I was not going to let my repressive upbringing sabotage this. There we were. Behind Skateworld. Life was happening. This was a big deal. And even though Sarah grabbed my wrist and stopped me from reaching down the inside of the front of her pants, it was a historic moment.

Thank you, Prince. You allowed my first real make out session with a girl to go off without any Christian bullshit sabotaging my fun. This was it—the spark that lit the fuse that eventually detonated the walls that I had built up over the years from repressive religion. I wanted more. A lot more. And thanks to Prince I would go on to reap a lot more torrid face-sucking sessions.

During those years, Prince came to my rescue quite a bit. Take the *Lovesexy* album. It's far from my favorite album and is generally considered to be the start of Prince's less creative period. A lot of his songs started to sound the same or just flat out bland after the triumph of *Sign O the Times*. After that album, Prince emerged in

1988 with this poppy, blatantly spiritual personal album that saw him looking at his religious faith with a newfound seriousness. Featuring a nude photo of Prince on the cover surrounded by flowers with phallic-looking erect stamens, Mom about flipped when she saw the record displayed at Sam Goody.

"Oh, that's disgusting! I can't believe they would be allowed to sell an album like that," Mom exclaimed. But actually, a lot of retailers DIDN'T sell the album directly because of the cover—it was like the *Smell the Glove* scene from "This Is Spinal Tap" or something. A few years later, Prince told Rolling Stone writer Neal Karlan that the Lovesexy cover was supposed to be about "vulnerability." It's easy to see what he's talking about. There's nothing sexual about the image, except for the aroused flowers in the background and if you can jerk off to that, you're a sicker puppy than even me.

The album contained a bona fide hit with "Alphabet Street," a funky and fun number featuring a cool rap bridge from Cat Glover, who had appeared in the "Sign O the Times" movie. Other songs like "Glam Slam" and "I Wish U Heaven" were also released as singles, but neither of them really charted. But *Lovesexy* saved my life once.

Literally.

I was 17 going on 18 during my senior year. This was supposed to be the year it all fell into place. I would finally tame my stutter, I would make new friends and maybe finally accepted into some kind of social sect—maybe the drama kids. I would write for the school paper and become editor, learn about leadership. I'd no longer let myself be belittled at home, or by rude teachers, and especially by my popular classmates.

None of that had happened.

In fact, my stutter was worse than ever, I was too socially awkward for even the drama kids and the computer programmers, and life at home was still a gauntlet. Despite my age, I still got spankings and if Mom got mad at me, I was barked at to "Go to bed!" At 17, I was a child. I'd had it. I was tired of coming home from school every day, going to bed, and then waking up to the same nightmare. So I started thinking about killing myself. I had a razor-sharp fish filet knife that my uncle had bought for me. I decided to run a hot bath and cut my wrists under the water. I'd heard it hurt less and certainly it would be less messy.

I got as far as running the water in the downstairs bathtub. But as the water poured into the tub, all sorts of thoughts began racing through my head. What if one day, maybe sooner than I thought, I wasn't the social leper I was at school? For crying out loud, this was senior year. A few more months and I'd probably never see most of the bullies who regularly made my life hell.

As my conscience gave itself a pep talk, I sat on the edge of my bed, toying with the knife. I could hear the water continuing to rush into the tub. Soon I had to make a literal life or death decision. My heart was beating so hard it was starting to hurt. I needed someone to talk to. But whom? I didn't want to call Chris; he may have been my best friend but I didn't think he would understand. He wasn't a real touchy-feely guy and right now I needed to be comforted. My cry for help went to the only man who was always there for me: Prince.

I got up and went to the boom box that sat upon my dresser. There were two tapes in front of the speaker—U2's *Rattle and Hum* and Prince's *Lovesexy*. Even though it wasn't my favorite album—or even one I liked all that much—I went with *Lovesexy*. Side A. I pressed play.

"Glam Slam" was just ending and the stirring ballad "Anna Stesia" was just starting up. I listened to the lyrics while looking at the knife laying on the end of my bed, Prince's sad voice asking the listener if they had ever felt so lonely that they felt like they were the only person in the world.

Wow. Yes, Prince, I certainly did feel that way. Damn. As the song went on, I listened intently; it was like Prince was singing just for me. The song goes on for a bit and Prince seemingly prostrates himself before God, begging Jesus to forgive him for his sins but also imploring him to take the pain away. The song is completely unpreachy despite Prince singing very explicitly about the Father, the Son, and the Holy Spirit.

I started to cry. I put the knife back into its sheath and threw it into my closet. Tears continued to run down my face as the song's crescendo kicked in.

In all the years I'd been going to church, this was the only time I felt connected to some kind of higher power. Looking back, it was probably just the positive endorphins released by my brain as a result of listening to good music. But at the time, it felt like I'd experienced something resembling a spiritual experience. Even then I was fairly certain that God wasn't talking to me; it was just my id or superego bitch slapping me a bit and telling me to pull my head out of my ass. But whatever it was, it worked. I didn't kill myself that night. And it was because of an obscure Prince song on an album that flopped.

V.

I was about halfway through senior year and I was confused. A lot of my friends were applying to colleges and universities, making plans to leave the Longview area and start new lives. But Mom and Dad and I had never had a single discussion about college. So I decided to bring it up.

"Well, Dad, I graduate this year," I said to him one day.

"Yeah? So?"

"Well, what about college?" I asked, with a sinking feeling in the pit of my stomach that this was not going to go my way.

"What ABOUT college?" he asked, raising his voice.

"Well," I asked timidly. "A lot of my friends are going away to college. Their parents are paying for it and everything, so…"

Dad cut me off and laid into me. "That's not MY responsibility."

"But, Dad…"

"I'm not paying a dime for your college," he said. "You want to go, you can pay for it."

After Dad said that, I went to the guidance counselor's office at school and got some Pell grant and student loan forms. I filled them out as much as I could, but there were whole sections of the application that called for Dad to enter his financial information.

But Dad was always a cloistered, secretive man. We always had an unlisted phone number, and in fact, we'd get in trouble if we gave our phone number out to friends.

So now I couldn't go to college. I was working at Taco Bell in the evenings and was starting to pay for my own clothes, food, and entertainment. When I broached the subject with Dad again, he dismissed me with a wave of his hand, and told me to pay for it with the money I was making at Taco Bell.

But Dad's attitude made me realize something that I had never noticed before—he couldn't figure out what kind of father he wanted to be. Did he want to be the hard-as-hickory disciplinarian that the Bible demanded and that HIS father was like? Or did he want to tap into some '60s Dr. Spock vein and be a more nurturing type? I was starting to realize that the beatings I had endured as a kid and getting grounded for relatively small infractions resulted in part from the fact that all those years of attending a fundamentalist Pentecostal church had downright warped Mom and Dad's view of the world and of parenting. Something told me that if Dad had never got sucked into the whole evangelical bit, he wouldn't have been as abusive. It was too late to fix anything, but I kind of forgave my parents for the abuse disguised as corporal punishment. They had no idea what they were doing. And this flap over not helping me with college was just another symptom of their uncertainty and confusion. They were brainwashed. Pure and simple.

I'll never forget this one Saturday in February of 1994. Dad had to go to the hardware store in Longview and I asked to ride with him so I could go by Just Music and buy Chris a cassette of Snoop Doggy Dogg's *Doggystyle* for his upcoming birthday. Just Music was located at the Triangle Mall not too far from the hardware store. No big deal. Dad parked his truck and we agreed to meet back there in the parking lot. I went to the music store, bought my best friend his tape, and headed back out towards the parking lot.

The truck was gone.

I went into a panic. As long as I could remember, I'd always been terrified of being left behind or abandoned; it was the reason I used to throw such a screaming fit whenever Mom used to drop me off a preschool when I was a kid. I had this deeply rooted fear of abandonment that likely stemmed from my adoption, though it would be years before I would make that connection.

Fuck! Where was Dad?! I looked around frantically, feeling my heart start to race. As I went into a fight-or-flight response, I suddenly saw the welcome sight of Dad's truck driving towards me. I ran towards the truck, meeting him halfway. I got into the cab of the truck completely out of breath, both from running and from panic.

"Thank God you're here" I panted. "I didn't see you and I got scared."

Dad chortled. "I just thought I'd pick you up at the store. What, did you think I was just going to abandon you?"

The answer erupted directly from my subconscious. I didn't even think about what I was saying—I just blurted it out. "Yes, I did."

Suddenly, Dad's face twisted into a mask of rage.

"You know what? Fuck you!" he shouted at me. I looked at him, perplexed. I didn't know why I had said what I did to him; it just came out from the deepest, darkest recesses of my soul. But why in the hell was Dad so pissed off about it?

"You ungrateful little shit!" Dad screamed at me as he drove his truck down Ocean Beach Highway. "You seriously think I'd fucking leave you? After all I fucking do for you!?" Holy shit. I had never seen him so enraged. And I was deeply confused as to what it was about my fear of abandonment that set him off so much.

That was the longest ride in a vehicle of my life. When he wasn't shouting at me, he sat there seething in the driver's seat. The cab of that pickup truck was practically filled with the smoke that was coming out of Dad's ears. I was confused and I had never been more terrified in my life.

When we finally got home, Mom joined Dad in screaming at me about my "attitude." I tried vainly to explain that I didn't know why I said what I did, but neither of them wanted to hear it. They weren't interested in reasons or excuses. They just demanded to know why

I "had a chip on my shoulder." The possibility that I was living with depression or some other as-yet-undiagnosed mental illness was never considered. After that I was grounded for a week, and while Dad eventually started speaking to me again, I never could figure out why he got so angry that day.

I continued to work at Taco Bell and prepare for graduating from Kelso High School. That summer as my friends were packing their bags and trunks and getting ready to start their freshman year at various universities, I ended up saving all of my meager paychecks for tuition at the local community college, Lower Columbia College, or Last Chance College, as it was popularly known. At the end of the summer, I had about $1600, enough for a few credits of classes and books.

The summer of '94 was so depressing. Not only was I having to save ever nickel I earned for college classes, I was stuck in a nihilistic haze from being broken-hearted. This girl that I liked, Hillari, ended up going out with Chris instead of me and Chris joined the Army right after graduation. My best friend was now out of my life and onto bigger and better things (though in a weird twist, Hillari and I became great friends in the late '90s and she once bought me a life-sized cardboard cutoff standee of Prince for a birthday present).

In August of that year, Prince released the *Come* album, which perked an otherwise dismal period up a little bit. I bought the album one hot August day when my Uncle Jerry, Aunt Loretta, and cousin Brandon came up for a visit from California. I fondly remember getting ready for work at Taco Bell, while listening to *Come*, enjoying the epic and sexy title track in which Prince describes his oral sex technique. Eating pussy never sounded so glamorous. Many of the songs had been featured in a stage show that Prince performed at his Glam Slam nightclubs, but as I didn't have access to anyone who dealt bootlegs, I didn't know that at the time.

The album cover showed Prince standing in front of this big, spooky, gothic -looking church with the cryptic note 1958-1993 under his name. I later found out that Prince wanted to release *Come* and the subsequent album *The Gold Experience* at the same time— one attributed to Prince, one attributed to his symbol name. Fact: This guy was just too fast thinking and revolutionary for a major label like Warner Brothers, I don't care how much they were paying him.

Come is a great album, though it was dissed by critics (only two-and-a-half stars, Rolling Stone?). The album gave Prince one of his last Billboard charting hits with the song "Letitgo," a mid-tempo number featuring the great Eric Leeds on flute, featuring lyrics about how Prince was trying to be less of a control freak. It was pretty astonishing coming from a man who didn't allow journalists to take notebooks or tape recorders into interviews.

But for me the emotional epicenter of the *Come* album is the song "Papa." Prince had basically written an account of the underbelly of my childhood. The song describes a four-year-old kid who is locked in the closet and later beaten by his dad for throwing rocks at cars. Sparse, dark, and somber with thunder sound effects, "Papa" is propelled forward by Prince yelling "Smack!" to describe the blows that the father inflicts upon the kid. When I heard "Papa," it was like every lyric was a shot from a music video I was filming in my head.

SMACK! SMACK!

There's Dad working at his drafting table, feverishly penciling lines and circles on project site blueprints.

SMACK! SMACK!

There's Dad working out on the lawn. Every weekend. Like clockwork.

SMACK! SMACK!

There's Dad chasing me into my room, shutting the door, the buckle of his belt making that unmistakable jingling sound as he snapped it off his waist. It was a greenish brown alligator skin belt that he bought at The Wharf in Ventura. I'll never forget the way that belt stung.

SMACK! SMACK!

Dad sometimes got this weird smile on his face when I pleaded and begged him not to spank me.

SMACK! SMACK!

8 years old. Bedroom. "Return of the Jedi" poster on the wall. The belt comes down on my ass and thighs.

SMACK! SMACK!

1984. Third grade. There was Mom standing in the doorway looking approvingly at what was going on.

SMACK! SMACK!

There was Dad hitting me in the face after I mouthed off to Mom about something. She commanded Dad to "Slap him!" And he did. Like some kind of henchman.

Child abuse is a recurrent theme in Prince's work. Child abuse figures prominently in the songs "Sister" and "The Sacrifice of Victor." Then there's the turbulent home life of The Kid in "Purple Rain." His dad beats his mom and Prince. When Oprah was interviewing Prince in the mid-'90s after the release of *Emancipation*, she asked him if his father was ever abusive. Prince's carefully worded response: "He had his moments." So, Prince clearly understood child abuse. To this day, I hear the song "Papa" and I cringe every time. But it hurts in a good, cathartic way.

Shortly after the release of *Come,* I started smoking pot for the first time in my life, courtesy of a high school friend named Ryan. I'd go over to his studio apartment and we'd watch David Cronenberg movies and get high. As I prepared to go to LCC, Ryan approached me with an invitation.

"I'm going to be moving to Moscow, Idaho. My grandparents live there and my family is originally from there. I think you should come with me."

Holy shit. What an opportunity. Ryan was an independent distributor for a multi-level marketing company called Equinox, which sold health products and water filters. Our plan was simple: Move to

Idaho, far away from parents or anybody else who could fuck with us and get rich selling Equinox products.

It sounded perfect to me. That day I went back to LCC and got my tuition money back and sold all the books back to the bookstore. Later that night, after I got home from work, I told Mom and Dad I was moving to Idaho. I didn't ask, I told them.

"But what about school?" Dad asked incredulously.

"Yeah, what about school?" I shot back, feeling confident that Dad, for once, didn't have a leg to stand on about the situation. "I work all summer long for peanuts and I have to use every damn cent to pay for schooling that does absolutely nothing to further a career! I signed up for earth science! Earth science! What the hell does that have to do with becoming a journalist?!"

Dad just stood there. Mom sat in her recliner, also quiet. For the first time in my life, my parents had no choice but to listen to me. They could tell my mind was made up. I was going to Idaho. That was it. The end.

Two days later, I loaded up a few boxes and a suitcase into the back of Ryan's Dodge Dynasty. My brother, who I hadn't gotten along with since he was a kid, just rolled his eyes at me leaving. My sister, who I was closer to, was genuinely sad. We hugged each other for a while. I would miss her.

Mom grabbed me in a big hug and started crying. I hugged her back. I loved Mom and I knew that no matter what she loved me. Dad and I hugged and then did our secret handshake.

"Good luck, son"

"Thanks, Dad."

Ryan drove about six hours east from Longview to Moscow, Idaho, home of the University of Idaho. Not only was it my first time away from home, it was my first time being in a university town. Moscow was small but filled with cool features. There was a little art house movie theater. A nightclub called Xenon. A great independent book store called Bookpeople. An indie video store called Howard

Hughes Video that had an entire section devoted to cult films. And a ma-n-pa coffee house that hosted poetry nights and served a mocha milkshake that I couldn't get enough of.

In short, Moscow was heaven. Yeah, it was a small town, but it didn't have as much of the small-minded mentality that I got back in Longview. I actually saw gay couples—real-life actual homosexuals—walking down the street holding hands together. There was a pizza joint that sold large one topping pies for only five bucks, which ended up being the foundation of my diet in Moscow.

I spent much of the $1600 I had come with on a computer desk and office equipment, which Ryan and I decided we needed if we're going to get rich selling this Equinox stuff. I spent the rest of the money on my share of the rent. After a few months, though, we hadn't gotten anywhere trying to sell the products. I actually did manage to sell a few bottles of shampoo by going door-to-door, and Ryan's grandmother bought some supplements. I also managed to sell a bottle of vitamins to a guy who lived a few doors down from our one-bedroom apartment.

But those sales weren't enough to live on and the money started going quickly. By the time November hit, it was snowing like crazy and we'd had our heat turned off. I was bundled up in my coat, hat, and gloves inside the apartment, eating leftover breadsticks and pizza.

Then I got a call from Dad. When he asked me how I was doing, I burst into tears, telling him how the Equinox dream hadn't come to pass and that I wanted to come home.

"You need to come home and go to school," Dad said.

"But, Dad, how am I supposed to pay for college on a fast food salary? I can't do it. It's impossible."

"Well, I'll help you with school."

"Wait...what?" I swallowed hard. Had I heard that right?

"I'll help you with school. It's important that you go."

"But, Dad, you said you weren't going to help me before. Remember?"

Dad acted confused.

"What do you mean? Of course I'll help you."

My mind was in a daze. What the hell was he talking about? If he had agreed to help me with college, I wouldn't have come out to Idaho in the first place. I don't know what led to the change of heart and why he suddenly was acting like he had never said he wasn't going to pay for college. But all I knew is, I was cold, tired, hungry, and broke.

"OK. Can you come pick me up?"

"I'll be there next week."

Ryan didn't take too kindly to me leaving, especially on such short notice. He hustled and was able to find someone else to make up the rent, but we stopped being friends when I left. I can't say I blamed him.

Dad showed up in his beat-up Chevy Blazer, helped me load up my stuff, and off we went, back to Longview. I loved Moscow and didn't want to leave.

Just before Thanksgiving, I went to a shopping mall down by Dad's office in Vancouver and went into Camelot Music. As I always did, I made a beeline for the Prince section because you never knew if Prince was going to surprise you with a new release.

There on top of *Controversy* and *Graffiti Bridge* was something I didn't recognize. It was all black, except for some peach lettering on the spine. It was … no, it couldn't be. I grabbed it and let out a squeal. It was. It said so right on the sticker on the cover: Prince – The Legendary *Black Album*. Limited Edition. No track listing. No nothing. It was just like the album from "This Is Spinal Tap." The fucking *Black Album*. The album that was never supposed to come out. When I got back to my parents' house I ran to my bedroom and slid the tape into the radio on my headboard.

Prince recorded *The Black Album* in '87-'88 and it was supposed to come out after *Sign O The Times*. But on the eve of the album's release, Prince had an epiphany, supposedly while tripping on ecstasy, that the album was "evil." He told Warner Brothers to pull the album from release, which they did, but not before a handful of promo releases got distributed. Those original promos got heavily dubbed and *The Black Album* has gone down in music history for being one of the most bootlegged albums of all time. Those original promotional releases that got sent out are now worth tens of thousands of dollars.

The Black Album opens with a funk jam called "Le Grind," which was apparently written as party music for Sheila E's birthday. Not much to it, but it's a fun song. "Cindy C." follows, a lust letter to Cindy Crawford, who at the time of the album's recording was the big supermodel of her day. Again, a pleasant enough recording, but nothing Earth-shattering.

Then comes the first of two songs *The Black Album* is notorious for: "Dead On It." This is Prince giving the finger to a new genre of music that was just starting to go mainstream—rap. Prince wasn't too fond of rap when it first came out, believing it to be a lesser form of music that lacked any real musical talent to perform. The song, backed with a deliberately rudimentary beat, features lyrics about how rappers are "tone deaf." The problem was, Prince didn't really GET rap. And just like my parent's approach to life, if you don't understand something, it's easier to attack it, right?

The other song from *The Black Album* that stands out is "Bob George," easily one of the most controversial recordings Prince ever made. Prince records himself posing as a character of an impoverished ghetto thug who brutalizes and kills his girlfriend over the fact that she's cheating on him with the titular character, a rock star manager who counts Prince among his clients. Backed with a sparse, pulsing beat featuring handclaps and the occasional guitar squelch, "Bob George" sent a literal chill up my spine the first time I heard it.

This was Prince at his angriest and most raw; a side of him that had emerged from time to time on tracks like "Ronnie, Talk To Russia," "Annie Christian," and "Thieves in the Temple." But daaaamn, here was Prince singing in character as someone else and the result was truly unsettling. Over the years, I learned that the title was likely a combination of one of Prince's former management team, Bob Cavallo, and critic Nelson George, who was sharply critical of Prince in the mid-'80s for supposedly selling out to the white establishment. There are all kinds of socio-economic subtext to the song that I could elaborate on here, but I'd rather defer to the book, *The Lyrics of Prince* by C. Leigh McInnis, a master thesis on the content of Prince's words that stands as the definitive work on the subject.

So, yeah, *The Black Album* = Great. I hope someday it's reissued by The Prince Estate on vinyl, though that will probably not happen. The ads at the time of its official release said something like "It will be available for a short time. Then it will be gone forever."

As the year switched to 1995, I realized something—I was back home but I really didn't like living under Mom and Dad's roof again. I'd had a taste of freedom and I couldn't go back. Plus, my relationship with Mom and Dad took on a whole new dimension when I wasn't living with them. They respected me and there was a more equal playing field between me and them. They weren't quite as condescending.

I'd gotten my old job back at Taco Bell, which didn't please me, but hey, it was an easy job. I also moved in with a co-worker named Gabe, who sported a homemade Black Flag tattoo on his wrist. We became friends one day when Gabe out of the blue asked me "Do you drink?" Being only 19, I had barely had any experience with alcohol and had gone through high school without being invited to one party where alcohol was served.

"Not heavily," I answered instead of "not at all." Gabe invited me over to his house, which him and his girlfriend Chelsey rented with another couple, Joe and Angie. I went over that night after work and got royally stoned and, for the first time in my life, drunk. While Gabe was equally wasted, he asked me if I wanted to move in to help out with rent. I could sleep on the couch.

"Absolutely!" I exclaimed. I moved my stuff in the next day. I thought it would be great. I'd have freedom, all the weed I could smoke, and a good friend to live with again.

But living with Gabe quickly turned out to be a nightmare. Sometimes the two couples would have group sex in one of the bedrooms and it was loud, noisy, and impossible to sleep. Gabe also dealt drugs on the side, marijuana and meth. I wasn't familiar with meth at the time—we had never covered it in health class—but it looked like poor man's cocaine. One night I snorted a line, and didn't like it one bit. It made my heart race and I couldn't sleep for two days. And two days in Kelso, Washington is a very long time.

One spring day, I came home from Taco Bell to find out that Joe and Angie had moved out and had stolen my case of cassettes. All of my Prince albums were now gone. I was angry, hurt, and perplexed.

I decided to get a place of my own and found a studio apartment in nearby Longview that rented for under $300 a month. Since I didn't drive and had no credit cards or debt to speak of, I could easily afford that. Now there would be no more crazy-ass, thieving roommates. Gabe quit Taco Bell and we never spoke again.

My apartment was small but cozy with olive green shag carpeting that always ate any dropped coins that fell on the floor; seriously, when I moved out a few years later, I almost broke my vacuum from sucking up all the change that had fallen into the fabric quicksand over the past three years.

That fall I finally started college at LCC and true to his word, Dad paid my tuition. The deal was simple: I would get good grades and support myself and he would pay for school. It was a great arrangement and worked out beautifully. Now that I was on my own, Dad and I struck up something resembling a friendship. We regularly met at Shari's Diner for coffee and he often drove me to work.

Something else cool happened that fall: Prince released *The Gold Experience*, which is considered by most critics and many fans to be his best album of the '90s. It's notable for being the first complete work to bear the symbol name instead of Prince; in fact, at the end of one song you hear Mayte utter in Spanish "Prince esta muerte." Prince was indeed dead, just like the cover of the *Come* album had informed us. Now shit was getting real. He was no longer Prince, he was The Artist. And woe to you if you called him 'Prince' around us diehard fans during that time. He was "The Artist" and that was that. But for the sake of simplicity, we're going to continue to address him as Prince in these pages.

The album opens with the closest thing Prince had ever come to straight-up hip-hop, the club banger "Pussy Control." This stomper finds Prince standing at his most feminist angle, telling the story of a woman who founds her own company, makes a shit-ton of moolah all while sticking it to the men who try to keep her contained.

"Billy Jack Bitch" is also a jam, featuring a great sample from Fishbone, taken from their number "Lyin' Ass Bitch." ("BIH-HAW-HAWTCH!"). The song is supposedly written about Cheryl Johnson, a gossip columnist for Prince's hometown newspaper. Johnson had taken to calling the man 'Symbolina,' which did not exactly endear her to Prince.

Then there's the guitar heavy "Endorphinmachine," which was apparently intended to be a single at one point because Prince shot a video for it that was eventually released posthumously. The song is a monster-sized jam with a great, instantly hummable hook. It's probably my second favorite song from the album.

But to me the best track is the album closer, "Gold," which is definitely Prince's "Purple Rain" of the '90s. Long, epic, and positively soaring, "Gold" features the great Tommy Barbarella on keyboards, an awesome background vocal from Prince, and most of all an important message about how "All that glitters ain't gold." You can hear traces of frustration from Prince's ongoing battle with Warner

Brothers seeping out through the lyrics, and I'm pretty sure the song is about how his then recent contract renewal came with too many strings attached. Is $100 million really worth it if you're a proverbial SLAVE to your contract?

Shit, I almost forgot about that! This was the album that was out when Prince had taken to writing the word "slave" on his cheek in eyeliner. It was scrawled on with the kind of flair you would expect from the guy, with the 'L' and 'A' written out similarly to the logo for the Los Angeles Dodgers. A few years later when I was working at Taco Bell, I once wrote the word 'Slave' in the same font on my name tag to protest the fact that we weren't getting our breaks regularly. Strangely enough, I got away with it for a few weeks until my boss Penny noticed it and made me switch back to my real name.

The most widely known track on the album is "The Most Beautiful Girl In the World," a one-off hit from '93 which finally got an album release with *The Gold Experience*. This version, though, is different from the Bellmark single of a few years prior, featuring a totally new arrangement with added production and studio trickery that makes it sound over-embellished, as opposed to the gorgeous simplicity of the original version. "The Most Beautiful Girl in The World" marked the last time in his career Prince would really storm the music charts with a Top 5 single.

Another track on *The Gold Experience* that provides a strong glimpse into what makes Prince tick is "Dolphin," which closes out side one. Listen closely and you can hear one of the man's deepest songs; a number that's clearly aimed at Warner Brothers and the whole SLAVE debacle. The song, a favorite amongst fans, is vintage Prince. On one hand, he's singing about earthly, corporal bullshit like the cock-up with Warner Brothers, while turning to the ethereal and spiritual to save him. If he is reincarnated as a dolphin, a universally beloved creature, will The Man (in this case, Warner Brothers) be finally willing to accept him? And he again warns everyone not to fuck with him. He is Prince. He is funky. And you are not. Don't tell him how to do his thing.

I was finally going to college, Prince had a great new album out, and I had a place of my own. Life was perfect.

Or was it?

VI.

$\mathscr{I}$ don't care who you are, the first time you have sex sucks. It's awkward, possibly painful, messy, and laden with land mines of every sort, from surprise farts to leg cramps.

But if your first time involved using a Prince-brand condom— yes, they existed in the '90s—you can at least look back on your sexual inauguration with some fondness and laughter. It was 1996 and I had started dating a girl who was even more sheltered and ruined from Christian oppression than me. Her name was Danielle. Sweet girl. Short. Naturally curly hair. Cute. She looked a little like a young Kirsten Dunst. Her mother was just like Piper Laurie in the movie "Carrie" - religious to the point of literal insanity. Her dad, who looked just like Walter Mattheau, worked as a security guard and her family was dirt poor. They lived in a shack-like house in the boggy part of Kelso, just down the road from the trailer park where my friend Chris used to live.

I'd met Danielle at a screening of "Interview With the Vampire" in the fall of 1994. This girl named Alesha and I went on a double date with Danielle and her toad-like boyfriend Carl. Danielle and I made friendly banter and made a good impression on one another. About a year later I was feeling lonely. I remembered Danielle and asked her friend Pam if she was single. Turned out she was. I was glad she'd broken up with Carl and was available because I needed a girlfriend.

Anyone who grows up in a sleepy small town like Kelso knows what I mean when I say I couldn't be single or I'd go nuts. When you're trapped in a small town that you have no chance of getting out of, having a girlfriend or boyfriend becomes really important. If you're going to be miserable and have no life prospects, it's better to have someone to be miserable with. I'd endured a childhood and adolescence of abject loneliness and I wasn't going to go back to that. No fucking way. It was time to find a new girlfriend as soon as possible.

I started calling her out of the blue, and after being taken aback by my sudden interest, she reciprocated the feelings. Without any great fanfare we started dating. She wasn't into Prince at all, in fact, she had never even heard of the guy. I was resigned to the belief that there was no such thing as a woman who was into Prince. I was a proverbial island in a sea of country music fans. Including Danielle. She lived for Garth Brooks, George Strait, Deanna Carter, and other country artists at the time. We agreed that Patsy Cline was awesome at least.

Danielle would come over and we'd go to third base, but being a Christian girl frightened with visions of damnation, and weeping, and gnashing of teeth, we didn't go all the way. We spent most of 1996 going to movies like the Leonardo DiCaprio/Claire Danes version of "Romeo + Juliet" and the godawful "Striptease," which offended her Christian parents something fierce. They would accuse me of being a bad influence on their daughter due to the fact that I listened to "evil" music and watched "evil" movies. At this point, I'd had it with Christianity. I wasn't yet brave enough to proclaim "There is no God!" like Diana Scarwid at the beginning of "Psycho III," but I was done with organized religion. All it did was fuck people up. Me. Danielle. Everyone.

In Prince's world, 1996 was a big year. That summer he released *Chaos and Disorder* as a way to hurry up and get out of his contract with Warner Brothers. He was still writing Slave on his face and in every interview he did, he would talk about the evils of contracts. He couldn't wait to get out of the contract with Warner's and be free to release music any time he wanted to.

Chaos and Disorder is Prince's big rock album and it's a great one. Critics weren't exactly kind to it when it was released and it tanked commercially, but I loved it. The album sounds rushed, frantic, almost demo-like. It's definitely his rawest sounding album since *Dirty Mind* and the record seems to have been recorded in a state of "Here. Take this. Now let me out of my contract." The album cover gives a hint to the tumult that lies within. There's a broken Prince record with a shoe print and gunk all over it and the symbol is crudely scrawled in what looks like blood.

The title track is some of the hardest rock Prince had ever done. It's stripped down, dirty rock and roll with Prince singing about a world gone wild; it's the landscape described in "1999" just prior to Judgement Day—a world overrun with crime and lawlessness. Prince rarely sounded this pissed off in his music. Sure, in songs like "Thieves in the Temple," "Darling Nikki," and "Bob George" he was clearly inspired by anger, but "Chaos and Disorder" takes it to another level. You can tell he's singing through clenched teeth at Warner Brothers and anyone else who would tell him how and when to record. This was war. And it was ugly.

Chaos and Disorder also has the dubious distinction of containing the second worst Prince song ever recorded, "Right The Wrong." We don't need Prince singing country music. Hell, in '96 I was all countried out since I was dating Danielle's country-loving ass. Hearing the man sing in a Western drawl is ... no. Just ... no.

The album ends with the enigmatic "Had U," which has always made me wonder if Prince had been inspired by Nine Inch Nails' song "Eraser" from "The Downward Spiral." Both songs are basically a list of emotions related to a fucked-up love affair. Prince always said it was a coincidence that the last words on the final album intentionally recorded for Warner Brothers were "Had U" and the title of his first album for them was *For You*, but I'm not sure I believed him. "Had U" is so nihilistic in its view, so angry, so bitter. And *For You*? Had U? I think there's more there than Prince was letting on.

So anyway, it was a night in the summer of '96 after I played *Chaos and Disorder* for Danielle, who was thoroughly unimpressed, that we were making out on my bed/sofa when she looked me in the eye and asked me directly, "Baby, will you make love to me tonight?"

No way. Had this actually happened? Was I, Jason Webber, about to achieve the impossible dream of getting laid? It turned out, yes. And I had just the thing for the occasion that I'd been saving and never expecting to use: A Purple Rain Coat. Contained within a purple matchbook covered with gold love symbols, Purple Rain Coats were officially licensed Prince condoms. Move over, Trojan and Lifestyle, this was the real deal.

There's no reason to go into detail about that night, except that it was as awkward, strange, and wonderful as a first time could be. After that, we were a couple of rabbits, fucking each other's brains out every time we saw one another. It was awesome. Not only did I lose my virginity when I didn't think that would ever happen, but I was with a girl who genuinely liked sex. It was brilliant.

While it lasted.

The problem with Danielle was that she put all of her energies into having a boyfriend. She had no real interests or hobbies of her own. She liked country music and scrapbooking. I liked Prince and David Bowie. It just didn't work. But we dated for most of '96 and the first part of 1997.

While I was busy hoofing it out with Danielle, Prince was getting married. He and Mayte got married on Valentine's Day in Minneapolis. I picked up quite a few magazines commemorating the occasion. I was truly happy for Prince. He and Mayte seemed to be a natural match, with her dancing abilities the perfect complement to his music. They were each other's muse and that sounded like the most romantic thing in the world to me at that age. I wanted to have a relationship just like theirs. It seemed like it was a true story-book situation.

About two months after they got engaged, it was announced that Mayte was pregnant. I couldn't believe it! There was going to be a little Prince or Princess running around. The year went by really slowly as I waited for news about the arrival of Prince's baby and the release of the biggest album of his career—literally.

That November came the release of *Emancipation*, which was three CDs worth of solid funk. Prince had been wanting to do a triple album since the late '80s and now that he was off Warner Brothers, he was getting his chance. Each CD was exactly one hour, each with its own special flavor. CD 1 was mostly funk and R&B jams, CD 2 was mostly ballads and lovemaking music, while CD 3 added up to almost all drum machine-heavy filler, except for a few good songs sprinkled here and there.

Emancipation could have been whittled down to a solid double album, but even the tracks that miss still have charm. The best songs on the album, such as the epic, eight-minute "The Holy River" and Prince and Mayte's wedding song "Friend/Lover/Sister/Mother/Wife" rank among Prince's finest works. "The Holy River" displays an emotionally honest level of songwriting that he had never reached before. "Joint 2 Joint" is a fun, sexy funk workout, featuring tap dancer Savion Glover's feet providing a percussion solo. I wasn't a big fan of the third CD, but the disc holds the distinction of containing perhaps one of the best songs Prince ever recorded, "The Love We Make." A soaring, potent piano ballad, Prince performed the number at the last concert I ever saw him at. The song "Sex In the Summer" isn't really a standout track, but what makes it iconic in the Prince catalog is that Prince and Mayte's then-unborn baby's heartbeat is used as a drum loop.

Prince released *Emancipation* via a one-off distribution deal with EMI, retaining all the rights to his music. He also started to give more interviews than at any time in his career, even appearing on Oprah's show to promote the album. I asked Mom to record the Prince interview with Oprah and she obliged, since I was working at Taco Bell during the day it aired. It was so awesome seeing Prince so open, joyful, and forthcoming. None of the aloofness or iciness that had defined him before.

But the trademark Prince secrecy was still in effect. About a month before the release of *Emancipation*, Prince and Mayte's son was born with severe birth complications. At the time, Prince and Mayte were really quiet about it, not confirming or denying anything. The rumor mill was rampant but it was confirmed the baby was born with Pfeiffer's Syndrome, a condition where the skull is too small for the brain. Soon after, it was rumored that the baby had died or been pulled off life support.

The rumors hadn't been answered by the time Oprah interviewed Prince and Mayte together the same week as the release of *Emancipation*. When Oprah brought up the topic, Prince just said "Well, our family exists…it's all good. Never mind what you hear." But in fact, the baby had indeed died a week after being born.

The death of Prince's son Amir (the baby was called Boy Gregory by the press until Mayte set the record straight in her 2017 book *The Most Beautiful*) haunted the release of *Emancipation*. But Prince and Mayte dutifully promoted the album, swallowing their grief and not letting on that anything was wrong. I can't imagine what Prince and Mayte had gone through.

Every time I listened to *Emancipation* from that point on, I got sad. This was an album about hope and optimism for the future, and now given the circumstances, listening to it seemed almost inappropriate. Especially "Sex In the Summer" and songs like "Let's Have a Baby." Those songs weren't just sad, they were soul crushing. I felt so bad for Prince and Mayte.

In early 1997, I stopped seeing Danielle, although she still came over for a booty call on occasion. Around that same time, I started crushing on a girl at Taco Bell named Lisa. She had beautiful strawberry blonde hair, and beautiful brown eyes. She usually worked the drive-thru and there was definitely a mild flirtation between the two of us.

I went so far as to ask her out but she gently rebuffed my advances. She had a bad boy fetish and at the time I was too meek and "nice" to be her type.

But Lisa DID accept my invitation to be my date for a major milestone in my life: My first ever Prince concert.

It was September 27, 1997. Prince was playing the Rose Garden in Portland, Oregon on his "Jam of the Year" Tour in support of *Emancipation*. Not having a credit card at the time, I begged Dad to buy me a pair of tickets. He did. Actually, he got four; two for me, two for him and Mom. This surprised me. Dad and Mom going to see Prince? Huh. I didn't see that one coming. It turned out to be an unforgettable night, and not just because it was my first time seeing Prince. What made it really special was that Mom and Dad were there with me. I wrote about the experience for the local newspaper.

Parents Bridge Generation Gap by Going to see Prince
The Daily News, October 2, 1997

Could it get any better than this? I am standing outside the Rose Garden Arena, preparing to see my favorite musician, The Artist Formerly Known As Prince. I have just been interviewed by KOIN TV, I am clutching the hand of my beautiful date Lisa, and to top it off, my parents are standing next to us, just as excited as I am.

These are the same parents who would look at the mascara-covered, high-heeled wearing superstar when I was a kid and shake their heads in confusion, asking "Who is THAT?" Now, decked out in purple shirts and wearing excited faces, they are attending the concert with me—and they can't wait to get inside.

I am shaking from endorphins, excitement, but also nervousness, knowing that The Artist has been known to use profanity in his lyrics and present a stage show that's rather … er … provocative, I've got my fingers crossed that my folks don't leave the concert offended.

Not that my parents are total bluenoses. Interestingly, they have broken the stereotype of people growing more conservative as they grow older. When I was a child, like most kids, I clashed with my parents about our different musical tastes. While I rocked out to my Michael Jackson and Prince albums, they recited the Parental Mantra: "Turn that noise down!"

But now here we are, one big happy, adrenaline-high family. We finally go inside and after paying a visit to the T-shirt stand, we find our seats and wait for "The Jam of the Year" to begin. Chaka Khan opens for The Artist and while she has a marvelous voice, her stage performance isn't all that impressive. Finally, her act is over and the lights come back on so the stage can be rearranged for The Artist. I am quivering in my seat, much to the amusement of Lisa, who tries to get my knees to stop shaking. My folks sit in their seats, and I can tell they are pumped. I shake my head in amazement. This is unbelievable.

The lights go down and the opening bass booms from "The Jam of the Year." I rocket out of my seat, screaming at the top of my lungs, and waving my arms like a bird. My parents? On their feet, looking intently at the stage, mesmerized at what they are witnessing: The psychedelic light show, The Artist effortlessly doing a series of splits, and nimbly dancing on top of his purple piano.

The third or fourth song confirms the fear I had earlier. The Artist bursts into his rap number "Face Down," which is sprinkled with a few words that I used to get my mouth washed out with soap for saying. I glance at my mom, who is sitting next to me. She's bobbing her head to the music, slapping her leg to the beat. That's the reaction I was hoping for.

The rest of the concert is just incredible. The Artist performs all my favorite songs – "The Cross," "Girls and Boys," "1999." By the end of the show, I am simply exhausted. My black T-shirt is clinging to my body from sweat, my voice is hoarse from cheering, and all four of us are emotionally drained.

The fact that my parents attended this event with me was what made this evening a night to cherish forever. The generation gap is always especially obvious when it comes to matters of popular culture, such as music. When that gap is bridged, and music is shared by young and old (no offense, Mom and Dad), it is such a wonderful feeling. I left the Rose Garden feeling not like a son, but a best friend. Thanks to their presence, and that of my date Lisa, this truly was "The Jam of the Year." Or any year.

(Reprinted by permission)

That night was a milestone in my life. I had finally seen Prince live. There would be other concerts, but that one was special. But even though there were thousands of people attending that concert, as far as I knew, I was still the only person in Longview that liked Prince. Would I ever find a girl who dug Prince as much as I did?

I did. And it turned out to be one of the most uncomfortable situations I would ever face in my personal life.

VII.

$\mathcal{B}$y this point I was in the middle of my second year at Lower Columbia College, and as per my usual custom, I spent most of my free time in the computer lab either writing movie and video reviews for the local newspaper or, more often, holed up in the college computer lab, logged into prince.org. I spent hours in the chat room, just so happy to be conversing with other Prince fans. And like every avid internet user, I quickly realized an eternal truth about social media: Since you're basically anonymous and no one knows who you really are, you can be as cool as you wanna be. None of the people in the chat room knew I'd been a joke at my school, stuttered, or was 22 and too scared to drive. Hell, if I wanted to, I could've said I was the vice president of some big ass company and chances are nobody would've figured out I was full of shit; remember, this was the mid-'90s and "googling" was still unknown to most people and very few people even had their picture online. The net was still the wild west back then and if you were in a chat room and you wanted to see who the person on the other end looked like, you had to actually send them a picture. A paper picture. Through the U.S. Mail. With stamps.

And that is how I came to meet the young woman who holds the dubious honor of being my very first internet girlfriend, Selena, who taught me that too much of anything can be a bad thing. For years

I'd pined away for a girlfriend who shared my obsession with Prince and eventually I found her via the chat room of prince.org.

I don't remember what me and Selena first talked about when we struck up a conversation in the Org. I just remember that her chat handle was simply 'Selena' and mine was 'PacketMan.' I do remember very well her saying that she was using the computer lab at her library and that she had dropped out of school. That made me a tad nervous because since I was working at Taco Bell and pulling in a total gross income of $11,000 a year, I knew I wanted whoever I ended up with to be college educated; otherwise, it would just be concentrated poverty and at the time, I was something of a snob about education. If you didn't have a college degree, you couldn't get a good job. That was my staunch belief at 22.

But despite Selena's lack of education or even employment, she had something that no other woman I had ever conversed with had: An encyclopedic knowledge of everything Prince related. I remember literally smiling at the computer monitor as we would chat, quizzing each other on lyrics and having cheeseball internet crush conversations that went something like this:

> PacketMan: Did U check love4oneanother.com today? OMG! Mayte's starting a dance company? That sounds so awesome!
>
> Selena: I know!!!! Have U heard Mayte's "Child of the Sun" album?
>
> PacketMan: Alas, no. Does 1-800-New Funk still sell it?
>
> Selena: I don't think so. It's slammin tho.
>
> PacketMan: It's heck-a-slammin, eh? ;)
>
> Selena: LOL! U know it, baby!

On and on it went. Two young, dorky Prince nerds who were about 3000 miles apart. Selena lived somewhere in Michigan called Hazel Park, which after looking on a primitive Yahoo map, I discovered was a suburb of Detroit. Selena told me that Prince visited Detroit every time he toured and that she actually got to see him live around the time of *The Gold Experience*. She couldn't really describe what it was like to actually see the man live, on stage, in person except to use adjectives like "amazing," "awesome," and "slammin;" she really liked that word.

She also told me that her mom hated Prince and only grudgingly took her to the concert. Wow! Another thing we had in common! Her mom hated Prince, my mom hated Prince. Selena loved Prince almost as much as I loved Prince. And lo and behold, there was my first online crush. And it was clear she reciprocated. Soon we graduated from just talking in the chat room to writing letters to each other via email. Christ, if I could've proposed right then and there I would have. Our letters to each other were crammed with your standard gushing and corniness of your typical early twentysomethings who were still hopelessly naïve enough to be unable to recognize the difference between idealization, infatuation, and actual love. None of those emails survive today, but I still remember bits and pieces of them, like her beginning one letter with "I am literally shocked. I have never had so much in common with someone." In truth, the only things we really had in common was a mutual obsession with Prince and fucked up families. But I couldn't tell that. I just knew that I had met a girl—an actual red-blooded female—somewhere on this non-purple planet who dug Prince as much as I did and who seemed to genuinely like me.

About a month or two into our online flirtation, we decided to take our imaginary relationship to the next level—pictures. Selena wrote me a nice letter and enclosed two pictures in the envelope. One was a '90s selfie, where she had just taken her camera, turned it around, and hit the shutter, producing a mostly washed out image where most of her face was obscured by the flash, but had good clarity of her eyes and hair. Holy shit! She looked just like Claire Danes! The other pic had been taken in one of those little photo booths with the curtain that you'd see at Chuck-E-Cheese or the drug store. She looked different in this one; her hair was pulled back and she had thin early '90s bangs that didn't exactly frame her face well and her skin was almost deathly pale. She had a few cute freckles though and a non-smiling but still friendly looking mouth with rather thin lips that were covered with rather sloppily applied rose red lipstick. I was no Glamour Shots photographer but I could tell she wasn't used to wearing makeup or dolling her hair up. She wasn't unattractive per se but she definitely didn't look like Claire Danes.

But I didn't care. She was a girl. She liked Prince. A lot. And she had sent me a picture of herself which clearly meant she liked me. Maybe a lot. Then around the beginning of December of that year, I officially and oh-so-sincerely asked her to be my "girlfriend." I told her that I would come out and see her in three months when I was off for spring break and that I just knew we could make a long-distance relationship work. We had Prince to keep us together. I can still remember the opening response to her email, which I didn't get for three days, since I sent her the "will you go out with me" email on a Friday and I had to wait a whole weekend to get back inside the computer lab to check it:

Hi Jason--

O wow! A little red corvette just drove by! YES! I would LOVE to go out with you!!!!!

Holy shit! I had a girlfriend who fucking loved Prince! I can't even remember the rest of that email but I'll never forget the opening sentence. The next day when I got to work I told my co-worker Matt all about how I had an internet girlfriend and I even brought her picture to work with me to show him—I brought the Claire Danes one because it was a lot more flattering than the photo booth one.

"Damn, she's cute," he said, eyeing her pic. "So, you gonna go out and see her?"

"Yup," I boasted. "During spring break in March. I just need to save up a little bit more money for the plane ticket." By the end of the year, I had the money—I just skipped going to Just Music for a few weeks. I walked down to the travel agency a few blocks down from my apartment and bought a round trip ticket for Detroit International Airport out of Portland, Oregon. It was a big moment for me—it was my first-time booking air travel for myself and I was flying out to meet my internet girlfriend.

The year turned 1998 with little fanfare except I remember being on the phone with Selena when the year was about to turn on her side of the country. As 9 p.m. My time struck, we yelled "Happy New Year" together through the receiver. "I love you, baby," I said to her. "I love you, too, baby," Selena replied. "This is going to be our year."

Since this was well before the days of unlimited data plans, I only called Selena about once a week, careful not to talk more than 45 minutes and only after 7 p.m. my time. When we talked, it was usually about Prince and whatever we were obsessed with at that time, like "Who is Bob George about?" or something a bit more lascivious like "Do you think Prince and Mayte had sex after he played her 'Let's Have A Baby?" I thought that was a rather lame question—presumably Prince and Mayte had been boning long before that song was written, but it opened up an odd side of Selena: She was really weird about sex. She didn't like talking about it explicitly but then would surprise me with some PG-13 candor. She got rather offended when I once asked her what kind of panties she was wearing but then on a rare occasion when she called me one morning instead of vice versa, I told her I had to go because I was getting ready to walk to work and was about to step into the shower. In a shockingly lustful voice, she panted "Oh, God, I wish I could be in that shower with you."

Here was the thing about Selena that provided my first inkling that something was...off. How could a young woman whose self-proclaimed favorite musician was the living embodiment of sex be so prudish one minute and candid the next? If there's one thing about us diehard Prince weirdos, most of us are really into sex; big surprise there. But Selena seemed really weirded out when I would say something sexual. Then there was the time I tried to initiate phone sex with her; a story best left untold because it was such a disaster.

But finally, March rolled around and after convincing Dad to drive me to the Portland airport—which he only did after grumbling that he should've made me pay for some of my tuition myself since I obviously had some extra money—I got on a Delta flight for Detroit. It was March, 1998 and I was off to meet my "girlfriend" for the first time ever.

"Be sure and call us when you get there," said Dad as I grabbed my duffel bag out of the back seat of his Chevy Blazer and got ready to head into the terminal.

"Don't worry, I will," I replied, feeling the butterflies of nervousness start to flutter about in my stomach. Right before I headed into the terminal I opened the passenger door, leaned in and gave Dad our secret handshake. To my immense surprise, he used the ceremony to stuff a $100 bill into my palm.

"Have a good trip. And good luck," he said.

"Thanks, Dad." No matter how much of a bastard my old man could be, he could also be the most generous son of a bitch you ever met; he's still that way to this day. Since I'd spent all my savings on the plane ticket, I only had about $75 in spending money for four days in Detroit. Now I had $175; a fucking fortune to a guy with an income level below the poverty line.

I breezed through the security since I didn't have any luggage to check in and the pat-downs in those pre-9/11 days were rudimentary at best. I made my way to the departure gate and waited for what seemed like an eternity even though it was really just 90 minutes for my plane to start boarding.

Holy shit, what an adventure! First solo plane ride ever going to meet the girl who loved Prince as much as I did. I was excited as fuck...but couldn't ignore the gnawing feeling in my stomach that I had set my expectations too high and that something awful was going to happen in this small suburb of Detroit.

The first clue that something was wrong was the fact that my flight was delayed due to snowy Detroit weather. Having never been to the Midwest I was unaware of the phenomenon known as Midwest snow and how ruthless it could be. Thanks to the elements, I ended up landing three hours late in Detroit. After finally disembarking and walking up the ramp to the gate, my stomach was aflutter with nervousness. In those days, you could still greet people at the airport gate with all those ooey gooey hugs and kisses that open and close the movie "Love Actually." Ba-bum...ba-bum...ba-bum...my heart was pounding in my chest because I knew Selena would be at the end of the gate waiting. Arms outstretched, tears in her eyes, all ready to get me back to her place so we could put on some Prince music and make out for hours.

Instead, what I got was her very pissed off looking mother, a scowling woman in a faded Red Wings hoodie and an outdated hairstyle that had escaped from 1987. And standing next to her, a very thin, somewhat raggedy looking girl who didn't look like she had combed her hair that day. This girl didn't look anything remotely like Claire Danes. But it was Selena alright—she was wearing a T-shirt from the Love Symbol days with a picture of Prince holding his gun microphone.

"Jason?"

I gulped. "Yeah, that's me. Selena?" I asked stupidly.

"Heeeey." We walked towards one another, arms outstretched... and gave each other the most awkward, limp-armed hug ever delivered. That's because I was badly withering under her mother's still snarling gaze. What the hell was this woman's problem? Snap out of it, Webber, and wow her with your politeness.

"Hi, I'm Jason," I said in Selena's mother's direction, walking over to her.

"Hey," her mom said unenthusiastically in the unmistakable husky monotone of a chain smoker. She shook my hand and flashed me a quick what-the-fuck look as I shook her hand and arm vigorously. I'd been shown how to properly shake hands in the fifth grade by Mr. Hartman, my elementary school principal and I'd committed the technique to memory: Eye contact. Firm grip. Sincere smile. Strong pump. But my spirited greeting only seemed to annoy this woman rather than charm her. OK. Fuck. I'd try to melt her iciness later. For the moment, I had Selena to attend to.

I don't remember much of what we talked about as we walked to her mom's piece of shit car and piled in the back seat. I just remember her hand being soft and tiny with thin fingers. When her mom started the car up, which coughed and sputtered to life only after some effort, I heard Prince's song "Animal Kingdom" from *The Truth* album bursting from the speakers.

The Truth was an extra disc on Prince's 1998 collection of formerly bootlegged material *Crystal Ball* that was initially sold via the internet, one of the first albums to be sold and marketed online. It was supposed to be a treasure trove of unreleased jams dating back as far as the nascent years of The Revolution to the present. But *Crystal Ball* is pretty much a disaster. For one thing, the retailing of the set turned out to be a major clusterfuck, mainly because Prince said he wasn't going to manufacture the set until he got 50,000 preorders. Not having a credit card at the time, I didn't order it. Turns out I didn't have to. Eventually, Prince released the set via Best Buy and Sam Goody/Musicland as well as online and the fucked-up part was that most of the people who bought it in stores had our copies before the poor bastards who ordered their copies directly from Prince.

Not only was getting the album a pain in the ass, there was the overall wackness of the collection itself. There were very few outtakes from The Revolution era. Most of this stuff was from the post-NPG early '90s; leftovers from the Symbol Name years. There're certainly a few gems on this collection and the good songs are fucking great. "Ripopgodazippa" had been written for the movie "Showgirls" and is used as the background song in the scene where James, played by Glenn Plummer, dances with Nomi in his loft. Funny, funky, and sexy, it's a perfect dirty jam for a slick, dirty movie like "Showgirls." There's a great live version of a funk workout called "Days of Wild" that marks one of the last times Prince would release a song with profanity, and other great jams like "Calhoun Square," named after a shopping center in Uptown Minneapolis, and the sweet piano ballad "She Gave Her Angels," about his love with Mayte. But despite a few good moments, the collection is mostly a bloated, padded bra of a compilation. Us fans wanted the rare shit from The Revolution or stuff from his really early years. But instead all we got was a half-assed pastiche of remixes, lesser outtakes, and filler.

And we got *The Truth*, which is notable for being Prince's lone all-acoustic album. It's raw, sounds like a demo—almost in a *Dirty Mind* vein—and is overall pretty fair. Not great, but it shows a side of Prince that we don't see enough ... him being a guitar hero. It's awesome hearing him pluck those guitar strings with such ferocity and on most songs, it's just him and his voice.

But the song "Animal Kingdom," Prince's preachy hymn to veganism, is pretty weak. His voice is fed through a vocoder, or AutoTune, or something and it's got this weird robotic tone to it that is just grating. It was this song that would be playing the first time I shared a Princely moment with my first Prince girlfriend.

"Man, I love this album but I don't like this song," I whispered to Selena, who held onto my hand in the backseat but didn't really say anything. I couldn't tell if she was shy or scared.

"But it's about how he doesn't eat meat, fish, or drink milk," she replied, then was quiet again.

I swallowed the brief urge to say "no duh" and instead offered "Well, I know what it's about. I'm just saying I think it's a kinda lame song. I don't like that weird effect on this voice."

Selena didn't answer. But I could sense the dark cloud still raining on her mom who was driving. She just seemed like she was stewing and me being me, I naturally thought I was the cause. What had I done? Was it one of those things where she didn't like anyone who dated her daughter? I really didn't get it. As I was pondering, it was as if she read my thoughts, because she suddenly started talking.

"Selena, I don't want to listen to much more of this," she rasped in her throaty smoker's voice.

"But, Mom, it's almost over," protested Selena, while suddenly holding my hand tighter. Her palms were a little damp but soft, as if she regularly used lotion. It felt good to hold a girl's hand again. It had been a while. But I was starting to feel really weird about the situation. Her mom acting like she was annoyed with both me and Selena. Selena's body language was contradicting. She was holding my hand, yeah, but she sat way over on the other side of the back seat, totally dashing my longtime dreams of being cuddled up with my Prince girlfriend while listening to his music. The moment was just awkward. But I held up hope that once we got to her house things would improve.

When we got to her house, which looked like it was about to be condemned what with the sagging roof and busted up porch, it didn't get any better. In fact, it only got worse.

The first thing we did was make a beeline for Selena's room. Selena was a 21-year-old woman, but her room resembled my 15-year-old sister's. There were crooked Prince posters everywhere, a twin mattress with sheets that were only halfway on, dirty clothes on the floor, and a TV on a dresser across from the foot of the bed. It was obvious that Selena was something of a slob. She hadn't bothered to pick up when expecting company. My mother would have flipped if I hadn't cleaned up my room before company arrived.

As I soaked all this in, I had another inner question: Where was I supposed to sleep? That lumpy looking twin bed was way too small for two people.

As I took in the scene and situation in the room, Selena clicked on the TV, which was tuned into Vh1. She didn't even look at me. What the hell? I had just flown almost 3000 miles to visit this girl who was supposed to be my girlfriend ... and she's barely acknowledging my presence.

"So ... whatcha wanna do?" I offered, as she sat cross legged towards the foot of the bed, watching the TV, which was showing Madonna's video to her then-current hit "Frozen."

"I dunno. Let's watch Vh1. Maybe they'll show some Prince videos."

I shrugged. "Ok, cool." I scooted up behind her on the bed. I wrapped my arms around her skinny waist and laced my fingers together over her tummy. I rested my chin on her shoulder and instinctively closed my eyes. My God. A real live woman. It had been a long time since I'd touched a woman and it really meant something to be able to touch a woman who was not only my girlfriend, but who loved Prince. So what if she liked Prince in a different way than me? Wasn't this the same girl who had talked to me about the Jesus imagery in "The Holy River?" The one who had made me a mixtape of Prince bootlegs? The one who shared my enthusiasm for the hope that someday we'd be able to visit Paisley Park together and gain an audience with Prince himself? Wasn't this...

"Hey, what are you doing?" she asked, her body suddenly stiff as a board.

"Ummm, nothing. I'm just..." I trailed off, feeling my face flush with embarrassment. I loosened my grip. But now I was really confused.

"Ok, what's up, hon?" I asked, trying to keep an even tone in my voice. "I thought I was your boyfriend. Aren't we gonna show any physical affection towards each other? I mean...that's what boyfriends and girlfriends do, right?" Her back was still to me and she continued watching Vh1.

"Hey...a little eye contact," I said, gently pulling back on her shoulder to see if she would face me. She twisted her body towards me and scooted her butt back a little bit on the bed, fully turning to face me. Progress! I leaned in slowly but determinedly, making it obvious I was going in for the kiss. She looked up into my face, pursed her lips together, and greeted my mouth with hers. Holy shit! I got a kiss out of her. I was kissing my Prince girlfriend! A real-life action flesh and blood female human who liked Prince. There was no tongue action or anything—it was almost like kissing a relative. Lean in. Peck. Pull back.

And it was at that moment that shit suddenly got really weird.

After we had exchanged our chaste, junior-high-level kiss, she suddenly lunged off the side of the bed to grab a pad and paper that was on the floor. "Hold on! I have to write this down!"

Write WHAT down? What the hell was happening now? The answer left me slack jawed.

Moments after the kiss, Vh1 had started showing a 20-second spot for Prince's *Crystal Ball* collection. I thought that was pretty cool, since I hadn't seen a Prince album advertised on TV in about six years when ABC showed a small spot for the Love Symbol album during late night. But what the hell was Selena doing? I saw her check her digital clock radio near on her scuffed and battered nightstand and suddenly write down the time and date.

"What are you doing?" I asked, confused.

"I'm writing down the exact time that the *Crystal Ball* commercial shows," she replied matter-of-factly.

"Oh-kaaay," I said, genuinely perplexed. "What for?"

She continued to stare at the TV after the spot had aired and the video for Wyclef Jean's "Gone 'Til November" had started to play.

"It's for the book I'm going to write about Prince," she said, enthusiasm in her voice.

Hmmmm, I thought. Well, at least she's got some ambition to do something cool. I don't know how pertinent the time and date a commercial airs is for a biography, but she's thorough, I'll give her that.

Selena continued to watch the video for "Gone 'Til November" and didn't say anything. I looked at the clock radio on her night-stand, which was cluttered with junk ranging from pens to wadded up tissues to the issue of Ebony with Prince and Mayte on the cover from a few years back. I leaned back on the bed and pulled my legs up to pull off my Vans. I kicked them on the floor and peeled off my socks. I then put my foot gently on her back and started playing foot-sie, caressing her with my instep.

"What are you doing?"

She didn't look around to face me, she just continued to watch Wyclef Jean.

"Ummmm...nothing. Sorry." She didn't say a word, but the edge in her voice made me get the hint. I removed my foot from her back, stretch out my legs on her bed, and leaned back and rested my head against the bedroom wall, continuing to look at her red shirt and seat of her jeans.

Something was really wrong here. The whole arrangement just felt awkward. It wasn't the lack of physical affection; it's not like this girl owed me anything, be it sex or a kiss. But we had talked about how much kissing we were going to do and all the making out that was going to take place when we weren't listening to Prince. So far, the only thing that had her attention was Vh1.

The rest of that night only got odder and odder. Despite my numerous attempts at small talk, she wasn't interested. And the *Crystal Ball* commercial played two more times, and just like before, she grabbed her notebook and wrote down the exact time it aired. By this time, it was the early hours of the morning, and I was getting tired. The time zone changes combined with the jet lag had made me really sleepy. I started to climb under the covers of her bed when she stopped me.

"No, you gotta sleep on the floor. My mom will kill me if you sleep in my bed. There's no room anyway." I shrugged and deposited myself on the floor. Selena went to her closet and grabbed me a dingy, yellowed white pillow and a ratty afghan. I stretched out on the floor, which was covered with cheap, pilled-up carpet, and covered myself with the afghan which itched like hell.

I looked at Selena still sitting on her bed, eyes glued to Vh1. Well, maybe tomorrow would be better. Maybe she's just blown away by me being here. Maybe she's nervous about what her mom thinks; after all, that woman would intimidate anyone. I nestled my head down in the pillow and closed my eyes.

Yeah, tomorrow will be better. We'll get a groove going, and she'll be more open, and we'll find the connection in person that we had in the chat room and over the phone.

"Goodnight, baby," I called up to her on the bed.

"Night," she replied. And she still hadn't taken her eyes off Vh1.

I woke up to a bony finger jabbing into my shoulder.

"Time to wake up, dear."

Blinking my sleepy eyes awake, I sat halfway up. Selena was still wearing her clothes from the night before and Vh1 was still on, showing a video I recognized as that one big hit from Lisa Loeb.

"Hey. Didn't you go to bed?" I asked, arching my back, which was a little stiff from laying on the floor.

"No, I couldn't sleep. I don't sleep much," she said.

"Oh, that sucks." I got to my feet and gave myself a good morning stretch.

"Why does it suck? They showed the *Crystal Ball* commercial four times last night while you were sleeping," she offered.

Tired and already weary of hearing about the *Crystal Ball* commercial, I rolled my eyes internally and sat on the edge of the bed. "Should we get some coffee?" I asked.

"I don't drink coffee," Selena replied.

"Well, does your mom?"

"Yeah, but I don't want you to ask her for any."

OK, now I was just irritated. "What the hell do you mean? Why can't I bother your mom for a cup of coffee?"

"She doesn't like you," Selena said matter-of-factly.

Hearing those words hit me hard and bruised feelings quickly gave rise to anger.

"What the fuck do you mean she doesn't like me?" I demanded, raising my voice up an octave.

"Keep it down. She thinks Prince ruined my life and since you like Prince, too, that makes her not like you." Selena replied matter-of-factly, eyes still focused on Vh1.

A quick lightning bolt of pure rage flashed through me. I was pissed off at everything in that moment. Pissed that this girl would not stop watching fucking Vh1; I never wanted to watch that channel again. Pissed that her mom would be so judgmental towards me for liking Prince…just like most people had treated me for the last seven years. Pissed that she was acting so indifferent towards me and here I was supposed to be her "boyfriend." And most of all, I was pissed off at myself because I realized I had made a big mistake in coming out here.

I still had three days left to spend with her. I decided to just power through and make the most of them. After all, I was on spring break and it was the first time I'd had a genuine spring vacation in years. I owed it to myself to try to live it up. I was a college student, for Christ's sake. But Hazel Park, Michigan was a long way from Fort Lauderdale.

First things first—I wanted to find out more about this shit about how her mom hated Prince and blamed him for ruining Selena's life. When I pried a little, Selena was refreshingly forthcoming, and actually stopped watching Vh1. The simple version of a long story: Prince was all Selena had. She had quit high school and never bothered to get a GED. She'd had a job working at a gas station for a minute but quit because she kept getting sexually harassed by customers and her asshole boss; couldn't fault her for that. I also discovered that her dad had split when she was a kid and had molested her, the son of a bitch. She'd only had a few short-term boyfriends in school and didn't really have any friends except for a girl named Kara and a guy named Pete who lived in her hometown.

So, her Prince obsession came from her channeling all her energies and unreleased dreams into one thing. I got that. I understood it. But it didn't make it any easier to deal with. Over the course of the three days I spent with Selena, I was starting to actually get sick of Prince. Selena would find the smallest, most minute detail in something and draw a Prince connection to it.

We spent one day at a mall, mainly to get away from her mom, and she would look at the fonts of the store names and question whether they were written in the same typeface as a Prince album title.

"Is that the same print as *Emancipation*? … Hey! Look! It looks like it's from *Around the World In A Day*." While we were at the mall, we went into a Sam Goody and of course, we both made a beeline for the Prince section. Yeah, we both had mostly everything he'd put out at that point–though I was still missing For You and Prince from my collection–but it was just something you did as a fan. You knew you'd see the usual albums there, but you just never knew when Prince would surprise you. After all, I had no idea The Black Album was going to be released in November, 1994 until I was in Camelot Music and saw it there, and bam!

We didn't find anything in the Prince section that was out of the ordinary. Just your usual *Purple Rain*, *The Hits 1 and 2*, *Controversy*, and *1999*. But I did get a couple of dope David Bowie CDs that were on sale, *Space Oddity* and *The Man Who Sold the World*. And for some reason, Selena had a problem with this.

"I don't like David Bowie. He's gay."

"What the hell are you talking about? He's bisexual."

"Right, so he's sort of gay."

I looked at her with a disgusted look. Was this girl serious? My mouth was starting to feel dry and I felt my stomach sink even further, if that was possible. Now the girl was homophobic on top of everything? Please, God, just let it end.

"Well, not that it matters, but Bowie's married to Iman. And he says his bisexuality was largely just exploration. It was the '70s, for Christ's sake."

Selena shot me a dirty look.

"Don't take God's name in vain."

I stopped walking and just looked at her. "I can't believe that someone as close-minded as you could ever be a Prince fan. I mean, look at how many people think Prince is gay. My dad does."

"But we know Prince isn't gay," she retorted.

"Yeah, but they THINK he's gay. The makeup, the lace, the heels. You can't be a man in America, dress like Prince, and not have people question your sexuality. It's stupid but it's the way it is in this country."

"Well...I know Prince isn't gay," she declared, her tone indicating this conversation was over. Thank God. Hell, how did we even get on this topic anyway?

For the rest of my stay there in Hazel Park, we didn't get in anymore flat out arguments. But it was strained and it got to where I wasn't even trying to engage in conversation anymore. Instead, I just focused on staying active and doing stuff; anything to stay out of her room. We went into nearby downtown Royal Oak and went into another music store, where they had a bunch of Prince bootlegged videos. I couldn't afford to buy anything else but Selena picked up a copy of "The Undertaker," a concert film that had been released overseas but never in the States.

We get back to her place and on the way to her bedroom, I made brief eye contact with her mother, who was in the living room, watching TV and smoking a cigarette. Once again, she shot me the evil eye. This time I returned her glare. I just wanted to go home. Hey, lady, sorry about your daughter but I'm not exactly having a great time here.

We got to her room and Selena ran to the TV to pop "The Undertaker" into the VCR. She assumed her usual spot on the bed and I sat next to her on the floor, feeling like a puppy. As for "The Undertaker," it's a very simple film of Prince and drummer Michael Bland jamming. It's largely just a curio for completists but there's a few great moments. Prince does a great cover of "Honky Tonk Women" and there's a fierce funk workout called "Poorgoo," which showcases some great work from Bland. God, Mike B. was such an amazing drummer. Still is.

But it was during "Poorgoo" that another classic Selena moment occurred. Prince sang a lyric that mentioned Trix cereal. And suddenly Selena jumped off the bed, exclaiming "Prince eats Trix! Prince eats Trix!" and ran to her closet and started rummaging around. The next thing I know her shirt is off and I got a glimpse of her in her tan bra; not a bad sight. A moment later, a shirt with the Trix rabbit on the front was over her head and she was positively beaming. "Like my Trix shirt? Prince likes Trix." I forced a smile. "Yes, so he says."

The rest of the day Selena sat on top of her bed watching Prince bootlegs and swaying back and forth on her bed to the music. I watched her, feeling an overwhelming sense of sadness. Prince was all this poor girl had. She had no career ambitions or any kind of desire to escape her situation. Her only source of happiness was Prince. I loved Prince too, but hell, I at least wanted to get the fuck out of my shitty-ass small town.

The next day was my last full day in Michigan and by this time, I was positively itching to go home. I was tired and grumpy from sleeping on the floor, sick of eating pizza (since we almost never left the room, all we did was order Domino's), and I hadn't had any privacy to jerk off since I'd arrived. When you're 22, such a situation is downright painful. But I tried to ignore my blue balls and focus on getting through the last 24 hours of my trip.

Since it was my last day and even Selena had gotten tired of being cooped up in her bedroom, we went to this flea market that she frequented. I heard a weird buzzing sound as I walked in, the likes of which I'd never heard before.

"What's that sound?" I asked.

"A tattoo needle. There's a guy back there that does tattoos," Selena replied, slipping her hand into mine in a rare show of affection. We walked along for a little bit, and I stopped by a booth that was selling used CDs and started flipping through the selection, finding the then-new cast album to the Broadway version of "The Lion King" and—in a rare find—the Roxy cast version of "The Rocky Horror Show." As I paid for my CDs, Selena suddenly piped up, "Hey, we should get Prince symbol tattoos!"

I looked at her. I thought about it. And then I thought about what my parents would say and how they would likely recoil in horror.

"I think that's a great idea."

We went to the tattoo artist, a grizzled old man with a Kangol bucket hat. Turned out he had flash art of the Prince symbol all ready to go, which was awesome. We decided that we would each get the symbol tatted on our upper arms. I nervously sat in the chair as the tattoo artist began to run the needle up and down around my shoulder. Yes, it hurt; anyone who tells you a tattoo doesn't hurt is lying. But after about 45 minutes, I had a beautiful replica of the love symbol etched into my dermis. I still wondered what Mom and Dad were going to think, but I reminded myself I was 22. What could they really say?

Afterwards, Selena got her ink, making me hold her hand while the artist, who was not one for small talk, did his skillful work. Afterwards, we both stood up and admired our new permanent decorative scars. After we paid the guy, we left his booth and headed towards the entrance of the flea market.

And then Selena got weird again.

"Wait, stop," she said, holding her arm in front of me.

"What?"

"I want to look at your tattoo for a minute." But the tattoo was still bloody fresh and covered with gauze.

"Dude, it's covered up right now. What do you need to see it for?"

"I want to see something," she answered, actually trying to remove the tape from my arm.

"Ouch! OK, hold on." Anger bubbling up in me, I slowly pulled the tape back, taking the gauze square with it, which now bore a perfect red imprint of the symbol.

Selena looked at the tattoo closely. I still didn't know what the fuck she was looking for.

"It sucks," she suddenly said flatly.

I sighed. "What are you talking about? It's fine."

"No, the circle at the top isn't centered right. It's crooked. See?"

Examining the tattoo, which was shiny with ointment, I saw she was right. The circle at the top of the symbol actually WAS a little off to the right. But it was barely noticeable.

"Oh, for Christ's sake. No one's going to even see that," I said, retaping the gauze back to the mark.

Selena continued to walk towards the exit of the flea market. "Well…I think it should be perfect."

When we got back to her place, it was just more of the same routine. Thankfully, I was scheduled to leave the next morning. The rest of the evening was just a blur. More *Crystal Ball* commercials. More Vh1. I basically just passed out on the floor while Selena continued to watch music videos.

The next morning, we barely spoke. I just got dressed, brushed my teeth, packed my bags and waited for her mom to get ready to drive me to the airport. I couldn't wait to get home and in my own bed. The entire trip had been a total letdown and, though I couldn't believe it, I seriously didn't want to listen to Prince anymore. After three days of being fed nothing but a diet of Prince and bad pizza I knew there was indeed too much of a good thing.

"Selena? Are you guys ready?" Her mom's gravelly voice rang out from down the hall.

"Yeah, we're ready," I called back, watching Selena lace up her Reeboks while she sat on the bed.

There was a pause. And then…

"I asked Selena, not you."

I didn't say anything. I just gritted my teeth. I could feel myself turning red. I wanted to punch a wall. I was sick to death of this woman.

"We're coming, Mom," shouted Selena in a shrill, piercing voice. It was obvious Selena didn't care much for this bitch either.

I slung my duffel bag over my shoulder and got ready to storm down the hallway.

"Hey, wait a minute." Selena stopped me. "Come here."

I turned to face her, wondering what she wanted. She walked up to me and kissed me on the mouth. And then I felt her tongue slither between my lips. Holy shit! I did not see that coming. She had never once let me French kiss her the entire time I'd been there, now she was initiating it? I kissed her back greedily, our tongues dueling together. I pulled away after a minute, needing to catch a breath.

"Damn, girl, why didn't you let me kiss you like that before?" I asked, putting my arms around her neck.

She looked down. "I don't know." I grabbed her in a hug and we stood there for a moment before we broke the embrace and headed out her bedroom door. Neither of us wanted to risk incurring the wrath of her mother.

We drove to the airport in dead silence, sitting in the back seat holding hands. No radio or nothing. I knew this relationship—if you could really call it that—wasn't going to work. I knew I'd have to break up with Selena when I got home, but I couldn't bring myself to do it before I left, partly because I was afraid she might flip out, usher me out the door and leave me stranded in Michigan.

But I was sad. I'd come out here with high hopes that I had found a girlfriend who "got" me. Understood my connection to Prince and shared the mutual passion. But I also wanted someone who had dreams, goals, and aspirations. Selena just didn't.

When we got to the airport, her mom just wanted to drop me off at the curb, even though in those days you could go to the gate with your departing party. Just wanting the whole sorry experience to be over, I got out of the car, retrieved my duffel bag from the trunk and got ready to head into the terminal.

Selena stood by the curb with tears in her eyes. I couldn't resist making a corny Prince joke.

"For the tears in your eyes…" I sang to her.

"Oh, I love that song! I wanna listen to it now."

I smiled and gave her a weak hug. I wanted to hurry because I didn't want her mom honking the horn and telling her "Come ON, Selena."

"Thank you," I whispered into her ear as we hugged goodbye.

"For what, dear?" she asked.

"Just…everything. It was fun."

"You're welcome." I gave her one more squeeze and started walking into towards the sliding glass doors. I looked over my shoulder and waved to her. She waved back.

And that was that.

VIII.

I broke up with Selena over the phone about a month after I got back to Longview. Years later during one of those "how-have-you-been?" emails we all send at some point to an ex, she bluntly answered that "I don't like Prince anymore. I'm into drugs and heavy metal." Last I heard about Selena she was living on disability in Carson City, Nevada. No idea how she ended up there.

So I was single and ready to mingle again and being the dork that I am, I went where the other Princely dorks were at: Prince.org. I was coming close to wrapping up my degree at Lower Columbia College and spent many hours in the computer lab talking in the chat room. During one such session, I met a nice girl named Sofia. Like me, she was a journalism student and also like me, she loved Prince.

I fell in love almost immediately.

Sofia was smart, gorgeous (she looked a lot like Mia Sara), feisty, and a good conversationalist. We quickly made the transition from chat room to emailing, to talking on the phone and to my joy, she had a thing for me, too. Unfortunately, she also lived in Detroit—actually only about 25 miles from where Selena lived—so I was once again in a long-distance relationship.

But this one felt different than it had with Selena. It was closer, more intimate. We had torrid sessions of phone sex, wrote each other letters—no texting in those days, children—and spoke on the phone a few nights a week, which saw my phone bill skyrocket. But

I didn't care. I was in love. And this time it was real. Unlike Danielle, and Selena, my relationship with Sofia felt much more real. We used to quote Prince and Smiths lyrics to each other all the time via email. Lots of "I love yous" and "I love you mores."

Yeah, it's corny, but, c'mon, I was young and in love. Sofia came out to see me for Halloween, which was our mutual favorite holiday. My brother, in one of his rare appearances of non-assholism, drove me down to the Portland airport and dropped me off. I stood there at the gate, my heart pounding.

Then there she was.

She was dressed in tight jeans and a grey Michigan sweatshirt. Big beautiful dark Italian eyes. Dark hair. A smile that could light up a bridge. She was a total babe. Everything I could have hoped for.

"Heeeeeyyyyy," she said as she gave me a big hug we'd both been waiting to experience for months. We stood there and hugged for probably like a half-hour, then we went to the car rental counter to rent a car. I silently cursed myself for not driving but Sofia didn't mind…at least not at that time. We got the car, drove back to my studio apartment, and another Prince-related dream came true: I had sex to a Prince album. Fact: Disc 2 of *Emancipation* is some of the best baby-making music out there. "Sex In the Summer," "One Kiss At A Time," and the great "Soul Sanctuary," which we considered 'our song.' It was unquestionably one of the most romantic nights of my life, even if we DID have to have sex on an air mattress.

The rest of her trip was kinda sucky though. Sofia got almost instantly sick with a massive bladder infection that eventually spread to her kidney; apparently it was caused by having a lot of sex after a long dry spell. Sofia spent most of her time in Longview in bed, because she was in a lot of pain. Being the trouper she was, though, she ponied up and we managed to go out to a Halloween party where I won $200 for dressing up as Austin Powers.

But leave it to my parents to fuck everything up.

Dad put a sour taste in Sofia's mouth almost right away because shortly after she got into town, he called me up and demanded I bring her over so everyone could meet her. This was during the short time before she got sick, and we were too preoccupied with fucking like rabbits to really think about family obligations. But that was the rub—I didn't feel I had an obligation to parade her around like she was a pet. I know my parents wanted to meet her, but one, I was nervous, and two, I was 22 years old. Why the hell was Dad talking to me like I was a kid?

When Sofia got word that Dad was being all pushy about meeting her, she wasn't really that thrilled about meeting him. Or Mom for that matter. But I was still under Dad's thumb—he was paying for my classes at LCC and there was a silent agreement that as long as he was paying my way through college, I owed him subservience. I hated it, but like millions of other college students who have been in the same boat, I gritted my teeth and accepted it.

But Sofia didn't understand that because she was paying for all her own college. Being 27, she was able to get student loans without her mom cosigning for them, so she wasn't a slave to her parent's wishes. Her father had passed away from Legionnaire's Disease a few years prior and was apparently nothing like my father. She really didn't understand my parents.

We did eventually go over to my parent's house and it was a disaster. Sofia went in with a chip on her shoulder and Dad, sensing it, was rude back to her. I can't remember what we had for dinner that night, I just remember not being able to eat hardly anything on my plate. Conversation was stilted, awkward, and forced. Luckily, we were able to avoid talking to each other by watching old family videos of when I was a kid, which made me really uncomfortable. I hate watching old family videos, they always gave me a weird panicky feeling. Much of what was shown in those old videos was staged and Dad would often turn off the camera to yell at us for various stupid reasons. Not happy enough, stuff like that. To this day, I refuse to watch old footage of my childhood. It's too stilted and too painful.

After a few unimpressive hours, we left my parent's house, and went back to my place. The visit had put a pallor on her entire stay. The fact that Sofia was really sick didn't help either. Still, it was great having her there and after talking about it for a while, we decided I would move out to Detroit after I graduated from LCC that winter.

I told Mom and Dad this, and while they were supportive, they were wary—even if they tried not to show it. "Well, why don't you just get married?" Mom asked me, to which I felt like replying "Because I wouldn't know a healthy marriage if I saw one." But instead I just said something like "We're still getting to know each other."

So the plan was set: I'd be moving to Detroit in January of 1999. I was both excited and nervous. I was finally getting the fuck out of Longview!

While I was waiting out the months to relocate to the Motor City, Prince's career was still in the toilet from a commercial standpoint. That summer, he released the album *Newpower Soul* under the New Power Generation moniker instead of his own name. This album is Prince at his most bland, a slipshod pastiche of would-be party music that doesn't really make you want to celebrate. There're a couple good songs though. "Mad Sex" is supposedly about Scary Spice, who Prince filmed an interview special with earlier that year called "Beautiful Strange." If you can find a copy, it's worth tracking down. Prince is really funny and flirty in it; I used to watch it to try to copy Prince's mannerisms with women—which always met with certain failure. Only Prince could get away with being Prince.

"The One" is a great, smoldering slow jam with a cool video directed by Mayte. The big surprise on *Newpower Soul* is this hidden track called "Wasted Kisses." This moody, bitter joint actually may be one of Prince's best songs of the '90s. It's unfortunate that you have to wade through a mostly throwaway album and fast forward all the way to the end of the CD to find it. Set against a G-funk-inspired background with a long, droning whistle, "Wasted Kisses" finds Prince sulkily asking rhetorically why he wasted his kisses on his departed lover. This song ends on an eerie note—the sound of a heart monitor flatlining. Some Prince scholars have speculated that this was the man's statement about his deceased son. I personally don't think so; I think it's just about a romantic relationship that's dying. Still, it's kind of a creepy song, though it's awesome. "Wasted Kisses" should have been a single instead of "Come On," the album's push for a hit, which is thoroughly unremarkable. I remember the video to "Come On" though—Prince dresses up like a street musician, with round Lennon glasses and a grizzled beard. He looks pretty dope actually, even if all it did was make everyone go "Ummmm…OK."

At the end of the year as I was packing boxes and shipping them to Sofia's house in Garden City, Michigan, people started talking about Prince again. After all, this was going to be the New Year's Eve of 1999—the year Prince had made famous. Radio stations were planning on playing "1999" around the clock, and record stores suddenly had a rush of orders for the *1999* CD. Even Warner Brothers put a sticker on new copies of "The Hits Vol. 1" informing consumers that the album contained "the original" version of "1999."

Oh, yeah, that's right. That weird *New Master* version dropped about that time. Prince, spying an opportunity when he saw one, decided to rerecord "1999" with his new band and release an E.P. called *1999: The New Master*. Featuring Prince's face on the cover as a robot, *The New Master* is a curiosity but nothing special. For one thing, the new version of the track is far inferior to the classic version that everyone knew and loved. You couldn't fault Prince for trying to cash in on the 1999 mania, but still, *The New Master* just isn't that exciting. It's got crazy guest appearances from beat box innovator Doug E. Fresh and even a spoken word track from Rosario Dawson (I've always wondered how the girl who played Ruby in "Kids" got hooked up with Prince). *The New Master* just makes you want to listen to the old version.

PURPLE BANANAS

I spent New Year's Eve of 1998 over at my homeboy Mike's house, playing beer pong and trying to act like I was having a good time. We listened to the obligatory playing of "1999" a few times and I thought of Sofia all night long. I couldn't believe I'd finally found the Prince girlfriend I'd always wanted and I was actually going to be living with her. I'd found a woman who actually wanted to have sex with me, be seen in public with me, and even cohabitate with me. I had arrived. What could go wrong?

A lot, it turned out. An awful lot.

IX.

I was in Detroit. And I was in love. For the first time in my adult life, I was happy.

Yeah, I was homesick, too. I missed Mom's enchiladas and I missed meeting Dad for coffee and pie at Shari's Diner. I even missed my asshole brother a little bit. Detroit was a great city. It was a culture shock going from a small-town hamlet of almost all white people to a Gotham City-like metropolis such as Detroit. I had only met a handful of Black people in my life until now, and now I was living among them. I loved it.

Getting used to living with Sofia though was harder than I thought it would be. As soon as I got to town, far from any friends or family, I backed into a shell. I was glad to be living with her—it's not a bad deal to wake up next to a beautiful woman every day—but I just felt like a fish out of water. When you grow up sheltered your whole life, dealing with serious adult issues can be disconcerting.

I instantly started failing at the relationship almost as soon as I got to Detroit (well, to be specific, we lived in Dearborn, which was just outside the Motor City). Sofia was working as a cub reporter for a small newspaper company and since I hadn't found a job yet I was keeping busy by putting together a spice rack for the kitchen, a coffee table, and doing other household chores. Having lived on my own for the last five years, though, it wasn't easy being told to do "chores." Plus, I told Sofia that I would learn to drive so she didn't have to drag my ass everywhere. But I didn't. Some of it was that I was lazy, some of it was that I was still scared of driving after nearly being in a car wreck when I was learning to drive with Mom years ago. Either way, I wasn't living up to my end of the bargain. This combined with other domestic failures had a quick effect on our relationship. Our sex life went from 60 to 0 in less than a year.

It wasn't all doom, though. I got a job as a stockroom manager at the local Pier 1 Imports, which I loved. Nothing but delicious smelling candles, wicker furniture, and cool décor. Looking back, that was actually the most fun I ever had at a job, even if my boss was kind of a prick.

But right when I was getting settled in, I got a call from Mom. Turned out Dad had been caught in the act of cheating on her and was leaving her to be with his mistress, who was 20 years younger than Mom and also Black. Her ethnicity was noteworthy because Dad hadn't exactly been an NAACP member as long as I'd known him. This was the same man who was not shy about dropping N-bombs and made no apologies for not being a fan of Dr. King or Malcolm X. When Mom told me Dad was leaving her for a Black woman, I actually laughed because it was so incredulous to me. But one thing that wasn't a laughing matter was how quickly I was caught in the middle of the breakup.

Mom would call me at least every other day to complain about Dad, and soon Dad began calling me every other day to complain about Mom. All this stress they were putting me under began to spill out into my relationship with Sofia. My already short fuse became even shorter and I started picking fights with Sofia over really stupid shit.

Then one night—on Halloween, no less—I got a call from Mom, who said that they were coming out to see me. They. Meaning her and Dad. I got off the phone perplexed, confused, and scared. They were in the middle of separating; why in the ever-loving fuck were they coming to see me now? Their timing couldn't have been worse.

I was trying to save my relationship with Sofia, which was deteriorating day by day due to my mood swings and lack of follow through on my promise to learn to drive.

Sofia was flat out pissed. "Why are they coming out now? And why are they just announcing that they're coming instead of asking? That is so rude of them." She wasn't wrong and I was just as pissed at them for pulling this shit. But all I could do was sigh and wonder what their motivation was for wanting to come out to see me at this point in time.

In late November they flew in and after awkward hugs were given, I sat down with them in their hotel lobby and laid it out for them.

"OK, look, I'm glad to see you but I really don't understand why you decided to come out here now."

Dad looked at me all perplexed.

"Well, we just wanted to see you. We missed you. Is that a crime?"

"No, but Dad…you guys are separated. And you decide to fly in to see me now? How the hell do you expect me to greet you? I don't even know how to interact with you. Either of you."

Mom didn't say anything. She would just wipe her eyes every so often. I hated seeing her going through this. Here's the thing–I didn't fault Dad for wanting a divorce. Life with Mom had been no picnic. She had severe depression and I was pretty sure she was bipolar. But he was going about this whole thing the wrong way. By Mom's account, he was basically trying to ghost her by living with his mistress and he wasn't even filing for divorce or legal separation. He just left. Leaving behind the dogs, Mom, everything. It was just a shitty situation, but I didn't grill Dad the way I wanted to. I had just resumed going to school at Wayne State University and Dad was paying for my tuition. I was afraid if I was brutally honest with him, he would revoke my schooling. I felt like a major hypocrite and Sofia basically thought I was a wimp. She wanted me to tell Dad to fuck off for what he was doing to Mom, and God knows I wanted to, but…I couldn't. And here they were. In Detroit. There was no escaping the situation. I just had to get by and pray things didn't get any worse.

They did.

Sofia still remembered the shitty, selfish way Dad had acted when she first met him and while she made a forced attempt to be cordial, she took everything that came out of Dad's mouth and twisted it the wrong way. Case in point: My parents wanted to take us out to dinner at a swanky seafood restaurant. Since Sofia and I basically lived on pizza and casseroles, we weren't in a position to say no. When we were leaving our flat, Dad opened the car door for Sofia and said "Even for you." I don't know how Dad intended that to sound, but to both Sofia and I, it sounded vaguely sarcastic. When we got to the restaurant, Sofia was angry. Livid, even.

"I am so fucking close to telling your dad to fuck off," she growled to me as we walked to the restaurant.

"Look, hon, I'm just trying to get through this. Two more days and they go home. Just please don't say anything. Please?" Sofia looked at me like she wanted to tear my heart out with her teeth.

Not only was that the most uncomfortable dinner of my life—I've broken up with girlfriends over dinners that were less awkward and stilted—but having my parents there even ruined the new Prince album for me. I'd gotten an email from Ross, the editor of the college newspaper, telling me they had a promo copy of the new Prince album *Rave Un2 the Joy Fantastic* waiting for me. In desperate need of some karma, I asked Dad to swing by the newspaper office so I could pick it up.

There was a lot of hype and hope pinned on the *Rave* album. Prince had once again returned to the fold of a major label—this time, Arista—and there was a lot of speculation that this could be the album to return him to the charts. It was 1999 and the big comeback that year was Santana, who'd scored a double Platinum album by teaming up with contemporary singers like Rob Thomas, Lauryn Hill, and Dave Matthews. Santana had inked a deal with Arista founder Clive

Davis, who came up with the brilliant idea to modernize Santana for a new generation. The strategy worked. Big time. Prince was hoping lightning could strike twice and he also negotiated a deal with Clive Davis and Arista.

Rave Un2 the Joy Fantastic features guest appearances by everyone from Eve and Gwen Stefani to Chuck D and Ani DiFranco. And in a weird what-does-it-mean twist, while the album was still attributed to the Love Symbol name, Prince—yes, Prince—was credited as the album producer. The schizoid nature of the album credits made critics roll their eyes. They were so sick of Prince being weird for the sake of being weird. But still, there was anticipation from the Prince faithful that this could be the album we had been waiting for. The one that would silence the naysayers who for years had dissed us for remaining devoted to the man Howard Stern now referred to as "The Artist People Formerly Cared About."

As I asked Dad to pop the *Rave* album into the CD player of their rental car, I felt a sinking feeling in the pit of my stomach. The first reason was because this visit from Mom and Dad was getting worse by the hour. The iciness in the car could only be broken by the power of Prince music. But I quickly realized this wasn't how I wanted to listen to a new album by my favorite singer. I wanted to be with Sofia, listening to each track and sharing our thoughts about each song. But I had to unite the three of us in that car into doing something besides talking as we drove to the MGM Grand casino, which had just opened in Detroit that year. So "Let's all listen to the new Prince album" was the best strategy I could come up with. Once again, Prince was saving my ass from my parents.

Rave is a solid album, but it's not the comeback Prince fans were hoping for. Though it was cool hearing such talented singers like Sheryl Crow and saxophonist Maceo Parker playing with Prince, who was never much of a "guest starring" kind of performer, the problem was many of the tracks constituted filler. There IS meat to be found but not every track on *Rave* is a banger. The title track, which had apparently first been recorded in the late '80s, was just bland. So was the second track "Undisputed," a weak rap number featuring Chuck D. But the first single "The Greatest Romance Ever Sold" is really good, tinged with Middle Eastern instrumentation and a great soaring vocal delivery by Prince. My personal favorite on the album is "Tangerine," which easily ranks as one of the shortest songs Prince ever recorded. Blunt, beautiful, and bitter, "Tangerine" is a message to a long-gone lover who still stirs Prince's heart even though he hasn't seen her in years. He describes carrying his ex-lover's picture with him everywhere he goes, but using it for a coaster. Powerful stuff.

Unquestionably, the song that should have not only been the lead single but a worldwide hit is Prince's duet with Gwen Stefani, "So Far, So Pleased." Featuring a great vocal harmony from the duo, this song was maddeningly not released as a single, supposedly because No Doubt had a new album coming out and their record label didn't want people getting confused about what album "So Far, So Pleased" was on. Stupid reason. The two singles that were released instead, "The Greatest Romance Ever Sold" and "Manowar," both flopped and *Rave* barely went Gold.

Despite the errors in how the album was marketed, it was a giant step up from the empty funk that dogged *Newpower Soul*. In fact, in addition to "Tangerine," *Rave* features another one of Prince's most emotionally naked songs ever, "I Love U But I Don't Trust U Anymore." Featuring Ani DiFranco on guitar, I remember this song reverberating throughout the rental car as we drove down Michigan Avenue and the awkward silence that it caused. Stripped down to only a stark piano melody and Ani's guitar, Prince sings about breaking up with his "protégé" and wonders "What happened to the ring that I gave U?" It's such an honest song it's easy to read the song about a breakup between Prince and Mayte.

And actually, that raised a good point—what WAS going on with Prince and Mayte anyway? About a year before *Rave* was released, it was announced that Prince and Mayte's marriage was being annulled because Prince wanted a relationship "without contracts." Fair enough, but why was Mayte suddenly living full time in a mansion in Mirabella, Spain while Prince was still living in Minneapolis? It was so weird. They were photographed together in several magazines at the time, including a really nice spread in the pages of In Style and they looked to still be the picture of a couple in love, but Rave is filled with songs about heartbreak and cynicism. Whatever the truth was, there was no denying that Rave contained Prince's best songwriting in years. I really loved this album. Too bad I would forever associate it with my parent's splitting up.

I decided to take my folks to the MGM Grand because they both loved to gamble and I figured it was an activity that they could do separately. So once inside, I'd hang out with Dad for a while, then go hang out with Mom. Both of them kept talking to me about their side of the story of the split and I tried to just listen and keep my mouth shut. But not so deep down, I felt myself starting to resent both of them. Mom for using me as her main source of support (she went so far as to call me her "rock") as she went through this and Dad for trying to get me to introduce myself to his mistress over the phone. I couldn't believe the nerve of him.

Thankfully, they left the next day and once they did, I burst into tears. Not because I was sad to see them go, but because I could finally unclench my butt cheeks and relax for the first time in days. We went to Sofia's mom's house and she fixed us her mostaccioli and meatballs, the ultimate in comfort food.

My parents' visit turned out to be a Pandora's box. When they got back to Washington, Mom had to move abruptly to California to go live with my Uncle Doug and Aunt Marion. She was simply wasting away with no support system in Longview, while Dad kept trying to get me to speak to his mistress, assuring me I would like her. Sofia? After my parents visit, she had decided I was a wuss extraordinaire for not standing up to Dad in favor of Mom. She didn't buy my reasons that I actually thought my parents splitting up was a good thing and that I couldn't just tell Dad to fuck off.

But the following year, I turned 25 and that all changed. I was finally at the age where I was able to get student aid on my own and didn't have to report my parent's income. It delivered a feeling of freedom I couldn't believe. I was free. And now I could tell Dad what I really felt about the whole sorry situation. But old traumas die hard and I couldn't quite summon the courage to tell him to fuck off directly. So I slowly stopped calling him over the course of a few months and eventually he got the hint. We didn't talk for almost four years.

I wasn't very happy with Mom either, but there was no denying she was the victim in this situation, so I stayed in contact with her, albeit on a more guarded scale than before. It would be two years before my parent's divorce would be final.

Meanwhile, Sofia and I were just coasting along. The salad days of our relationship were long over. Passionate sex and long deep kisses had given way to quick pecks and simple utterances of "Goodnight" as we slept with our backs facing each other. It was a shame that we'd once been the same couple who used to make love to *Emancipation*.

Thankfully, though, Prince still helped connect us. We both really enjoyed the *Rave* album, both agreed that Prince's final album for Warner Brothers', which was released to finish out Prince's contract—*The Vault*—was pointless. In fact, there were only two good songs on *The Vault*, a bright, peppy jaunt called "Sarah" and the official version of an old Prince bootleg "Old Friends 4 Sale," which now sounded overproduced and featured different, less powerful lyrics. *The Vault* is not really worth listening to. Prince totally ignored its release and by and large, so did the Prince faithful.

But one day in late 2000 I read that Prince was doing a brief Hit N Run tour, where he was booking shows on the fly and performing with hardly any notice. To my shock and delight, he scheduled a concert at the State Theater in Detroit. Though we couldn't really afford tickets, I'd just gotten my first credit card and begun my bad habit of buying way too many concert tickets, which lasts to this day. Hey, we all have our vices.

This was only my second time seeing Prince live AND I was seeing him with Sofia. We both saw this as an expression of the purple force that had brought us together in the first place. Maybe we could rediscover what we once had by getting baptized together at a Prince concert?

The show was amazing and filled my heart with joy. Prince, now sporting little pigtails all through his hair, opened with "Uptown" from *Dirty Mind* and played a lot of deep material that was only for the diehard fans. He did his version of "Nothing Compares 2 U," which he wrote in the mid-'80s, as well as fan favorites like "The Ballad of Dorothy Parker" and "Scandalous." Naturally he did the hits, but he performed them with such joy and zeal that it was impossible not to be moved hearing "When Doves Cry" for the five hundredth time.

A Prince concert was like getting filled with the Holy Spirit, except it was real. Every time I saw Prince, I came away inspired to make my dreams come true. That night as Sofia and I walked out of The State Theater (now known as The Fillmore Detroit thanks to stupid Live Nation) towards her car—holding hands for the first time in forever—I thought about all the dreams I still had. Finishing school with my journalism degree. One day writing for Rolling Stone and interviewing Prince for a big feature like Neal Karlan did. Getting out of Pier 1 and working in a busy, noisy, bustling newsroom where I was on the entertainment beat. As I made my mental list of goals that night, I realized that getting married and having kids was not among them. Years of living in the shadow of my parent's dysfunctional union not to mention their completely bizarre separation that found me caught in the middle had permanently soured me on the concept of marriage. I knew a lot of married people, but I sure as shit didn't know very many happy couples. I only saw people who were so numbed by life and repetition that the only thing they could summon was a vague contentment and resignation to their fate. The problem was I knew Sofia wanted to get married. At that time, I doubt she wanted to be married to ME—hell, I knew I was a shitty partner—but I did know she wanted to be married one day. Her parents had enjoyed a really healthy, loving relationship while her dad was alive and we just had been emotionally programmed by our vastly different experiences in growing up.

I knew by the spring of 2001 that things with Sofia would probably end at some point. I was really devastated to come to this realization. I mean, I'd moved across the country to be with her and I didn't really have a backup plan in case things didn't work out.

As a way to try and salvage the relationship, I started taking a few driving lessons from Sears and I also got a place of my own as a way to give us space from each other to see if that would improve the situation. Sadly, it didn't really help. We were just too far removed from each other. She even took back a framed picture of herself that she had once given me when I was in Washington and mailed the photo to some pen pal she had in Europe. I also found out inadvertently that she was talking in Yahoo! chat rooms under the name 'scarletf4u.' That's not the kind of chat handle one uses when they're looking for recipes. When I confronted her on it, she flipped out on me and called me a "spy." It was horrible.

But that summer, there was a brief glimmer of salvation in the form of yet another Prince concert. This time he was playing at the Joe Louis Arena where the Detroit Red Wings played. I got us great seats off to the side of the stage, and I even wrote a review of the show for the Wayne State University paper. It may have been too late for me and Sofia, but Prince allowed us to call it a day with big smiles.

Prince Returns to Form at Joe Louis Concert
The South End, June 25, 2001

"I'm baaaaack," intoned Prince from the stage on Saturday night at Joe Louis Arena. After a lackluster previous concert at the State Theater last November, the Prince that fans know and love is indeed back, and with more energy and feeling than ever.

With his signature opening number "Let's Go Crazy," Prince worked the stage as if "Purple Rain" had never gone off MTV. Thankfully, he performed more than just his greatest hits, which greatly marred his State Theater performance the last time he played in Detroit.

Now 43 years old, the Minneapolis wunderkind recently pledged to stop cursing in performances, and according to many reports, has become a Jehovah's Witness. So songs like "Sexy MF" and "Face Down" were nowhere to be found, which disappointed some concertgoers.

Prince has always called Detroit his "second hometown," and played songs that he has not performed in years. "Sexy Dancer" and "I Wanna Be Your Lover," two gems from his 1979 self-titled album, made appearances, as did some other rarely-heard songs like "And God Created Woman" and "Free."

Always eager to remind his audience that he can play over two dozen instruments, Prince took to the drums during "Sexy Dancer," and played four or five songs while sitting at his trademark purple piano. One of the highlights of the show was when Prince played some of his more obscure piano numbers, including the haunting "Sometimes It Snows In April" and the heart-wrenching "I

Love U But I Don't Trust U Anymore," which is most likely about his recent divorce from his wife Mayte Garcia.

Obviously in a playful mood, Prince enjoyed his rapport with the audience, telling them, "I'm gonna take my time tonight. Call a babysitter!" The man was as good as his word, playing for over two hours. For a performer who's known for a somewhat somber persona, Prince seemed downright happy to be performing. His enthusiasm was contagious, as the crowd sang along with every word and danced in the aisles.

"Do y'all remember a DJ named the Electrifying Mojo?" Prince asked the crowd at one point. When the audience applauded, he talked about how Mojo helped him establish his Detroit fan base, and about the monopolization of radio. While his comments were a bit preachy, it's easy to see while he would want to discuss music business politics with his fans. After all, this is the same guy who changed his name to a symbol and wrote "SLAVE" on his face to protest his old record deal with Warner Brothers.

After leaving the stage for five minutes, Prince reemerged to play "U Got the Look." He closed with his racy house-party anthem "Gett Off," which despite the absence of swear words, was still suggestive enough to satisfy those who longed for the days when he used to wear ass-less pants.

"I love you so much, Detroit," he shouted at one point.

We love you too, Prince.

(Reprinted with permission)

X.

$\mathcal{S}$ofia and I were done. As I approached my 26th birthday, I knew a change had to be made. We had gone a year without sex, I had moved out instead of moving in, and the space between us had grown ice cold. The last straw came about when I taxied over to her place just to spend the night, and she got mad at me for coming over without permission. In retrospect, it *was* rude of me to just go over there with no warning, but we were still a couple and I thought that was allowed.

It was exactly one week after 9/11 that I broke up with Sofia. That fateful event made everyone reassess their lives and I looked at the two of us as a couple and just decided that had to be it. Sofia took it well; in fact, I think if I hadn't made the first move she would have done it not too long after. But like a lot of my breakups throughout my life, I couldn't let her go entirely. We still tried to hang out and do the "we can still be friends" malarkey, but it was tough. Breaking up with someone who you move 2,500 miles to be with is a whole different beast than splitting up with someone from your hometown. But life goes on and I tried my best to get through the early 2000s. As usual I relied on Prince to try and get me through. Problem was, he was kind of at a creative low point.

The Rainbow Children is a preachy, eclectic album that was directly inspired by Prince's then-recent conversion to the Jehovah's Witnesses. He joined the church/cult/whatever after he started studying the Bible with Larry Graham, Sly Stone's former bassist. A lot of Prince fans didn't like Larry because suddenly Prince—the composer of "Sexy MF"—stopped swearing in all of his songs and started talking about the JW church like Tom Cruise talked about Scientology … hopelessly devout and rather tone deaf. *The Rainbow Children,* which carried a yellow sticker saying it was "The Controversial New Album from Prince" marked the man's return to using the moniker 'Prince' but also a return to the strong spirituality he summoned up on *Lovesexy*. Some folks got it, some folks didn't, and then there were people who "got it" but didn't like it. I counted myself amongst the latter.

A concept album with a muddled narrative, Prince tells the story of The Rainbow Children, putting himself as a character called "The Wise One." In between songs, there's a slowed down vocal, similar in tone to the Bob George voice that sets up the story. There really isn't much of a plot to speak of, but the main point of the album is that Prince wants you to know he's now a Jehovah's Witness. Musically, the album is very jazz-influenced, some of it really good ("The Work Pt. 1 and 2") and some of it thoroughly execrable (the song "Wedding Feast" gets my vote as the single worst song Prince ever released). But there's a really good slow jam called "She Loves Me 4 Me," which seems to be aimed at Prince's then-fiancé Manuella, and an epic closing song called "The Last December."

The Rainbow Children is a valiant attempt at saying something important, but not a major notch in the career of Prince. The good songs are great, but unless you're already a JW, there's no way this album is going to convert you. Kevin Smith was even hired to do a documentary about the album, the story of which is surreal and hilarious; it's available on the DVD "An Evening with Kevin Smith." Prince's spiritual awakening albums—this one and *Lovesexy*—tend to be among his duller albums. They're just too heavy-handed and too bossy. Listening to "The Rainbow Children," I felt like I was back in the Full Gospel Lighthouse. Not good.

Still, that album was a hell of a lot better than the album he released the following year, *N.E.W.S.* This is basically an all-instrumental hour or so of jazz noodling. I didn't like the album when I first heard it and it never did grow on me over the passing years. It sounds like a bad outtake of someone trying to channel Charlie Parker on jazz night at the local neighborhood pub.

Beyond the fact that it's just a pointless exercise in meandering, *N.E.W.S.* was also released at the same time that Sofia had just started going out with Glenn, a 32-year-old virgin who read Tom Clancy novels and voted for Bush. Glenn had one thing going for him though—he was the leader of the local Detroit Prince fan group, The Detroit Crawl. In a city where Prince was revered, Glenn was indisputably a big deal. As a Prince fan, he was like the star quarterback in high school. And yet, here was a guy still hadn't found a girl to pop his cherry at 32, but somehow, he was going out with my ex-girlfriend. I was jealous as hell. To this day, I equate *N.E.W.S* with the feelings of jealousy and heartbreak I had at the time, which is another reason I don't like the album. I've never been one to have an easy time with breakups.

Meanwhile, my own love life was turning into a cesspool. Being free from Sofia after a year of us not having sex, I was a little horndog who was determined to make the most out of my freedom. I bedded quite a few girls, determined to make up for the last three years I'd spent with Sofia. I even got a girlfriend named Sabrina, a nice girl who like me was Mexican and German, and from a family where she'd been sheltered much of her life. She wasn't much of a Prince fan but we bonded over a mutual love of "Jackass," sex (I was her first lover), and going to concerts at Pine Knob just outside of Detroit.

The problem was I couldn't stay faithful to Sabrina, no matter how hard I tried. After the devastation of relocating across the country for someone only to have it not work out, I couldn't take monogamous relationships seriously. What was the point? Everyone I knew who was married, from my parents and grandparents to Sabrina's parents, were absolutely miserable. At the most they were merely numb with contentment. I wanted happiness. And sex made me happy. Pure and simple.

It was around this time that I finally graduated from college with my journalism degree. Twenty thousand dollars in borrowed funds and I had something nice to hang on my wall. I even got a job as a calendar editor for an alternative newsweekly. There was just one problem—it was in Toledo. Rather than commute to Toledo every day, I announced plans to relocate 70 miles south to northwestern Ohio. Needless to say, this did not make Sabrina very happy. I was a total prick and tried to break up with her, doing the old "it was fun while it lasted" routine, but in all honesty, I knew I loved the girl. I was her first serious love and like all first-time adult relationships, it was really intense for her. Basically, I was to her what Sofia had been to me. That was a heavy load to carry. And I didn't carry it very well.

I brought Sabrina with me when I moved to Toledo and while I wasn't really thrilled about cohabitating with someone again, I wanted to make it work. I was employed by Adams Street Publishing, which was owned by a husband and wife team named Mark and Collette Jacobs. Together, they published the Toledo City Paper and two regional parenting publications. I wasn't making much money, but the job was everything I could have asked for in my late '20s—I got free concert tickets to lots of shows, I got to interview people I admired like Alice Cooper, the late Ryan Dunn of "Jackass" fame, and even one of my all-time heroes, Ted Neeley from the "Jesus Christ Superstar" movie.

The Toledo City Paper years were pretty great. Stressful, sure, but awesome nonetheless. I got hired by the Jacobs in January of 2004. By August of that year, I had been quickly promoted from calendar editor to staff writer to editor in a quick succession. It felt awesome to be able to call myself a real bona fide journalist. I worked at the Toledo City Paper from 2004 to 2008. And I equate those years with some dope Prince albums.

In September of 2004, Prince released *Musicology*, which was his first release on Columbia Records. Like the *Rave* album, part of the deal of working with a major label again was that he would own the masters. *Musicology* was heavily hyped and promoted well, and it was so cool suddenly having Prince back on everyone's lips again. He snagged cover stories for Rolling Stone and Entertainment Weekly among others, though he channeled L.L. Cool J by constantly saying "Don't call it a comeback. I never went anywhere."

Musicology is a solid album, although not part of the classic Prince canon. The point of the album was for Prince to school people on what real music played by real musicians sounded like. The title track is solid and funky with some great bass, and the sexy slow jam "Call My Name" ranks as one of his best lovemaking anthems of the 2000s, with great, sexy lyrics about how he can't stop writing songs about his muse because he loves her so much. My favorite track on the album is "Illusion, Coma, Pimp, and Circumstance," which has Prince singing in the higher register of his lower voice, making his voice sound strained and cracking. It's a cool effect. I thought "Cinnamon Girl" was a cover of the Neil Young song when I first saw it on the track listing, but nope, it's actually a thundering rock number about the second Gulf War, which was raging on during that time.

I remember when *Musicology* came out, I brought it into my office and we bumped it on the CD player. Our arts and entertainment editor Steve really liked it, especially "Call My Name," which he said reminded him of his wife. After playing the album around the office, one of the guys in the sales department went out and bought a copy, which he said was the first time he'd bought a Prince album since the late '80s.

For me, the *Musicology* era was really special because I took Sabrina to her first Prince concert when the accompanying tour came to Detroit. Just as Prince had dazzled and wowed my parents years ago, he blew Sabrina away with his performance. We had nosebleed seats and Prince and his band were mere specks in the distance, but we could still hear the music clearly. God, it was amazing. We had hit up the merchandise stand before the show and I finally bought the symbol tambourine I'd always wanted (today it hangs on my living room wall) and we also bought a teddy bear wearing a *Sign O the Times* shirt, which paired nicely with Sabrina's Melissa Etheridge bear she had on her nightstand.

The *Musicology* tour wasn't the best Prince show I ever saw, but it was a damn good time to be a Prince fan. The man was fresh in people's minds because that year he had been inducted into the Rock and Roll Hall of Fame—unsurprisingly the first year he was eligible—and he'd wowed the Grammys that year by doing a dope medley of songs with Beyoncé. Fit, trim, and dressed head to toe in old school purple, Prince was suddenly reminding the world why he became a star.

Plus, you know how a lot of times you'll go to an artist's concert and you get a free copy of their new album? Prince invented that. If you bought a ticket for a *Musicology* show, you were given a copy of the album as you went in. In those days, this tactic was so new that the music industry hadn't worked out the kinks yet and so every ticket sold also counted as an album sale. So suddenly Prince had a top 10 Billboard album again for the first time in decades. Granted, he only got it by exploiting a technicality, but more power to the man.

As the middle of the aughts came and went, Sabrina and I hoofed it out in Toledo. We each made a new group of friends, some mutual, some not, and I did my best to stay faithful to her. God bless that girl for putting up with my still-undiagnosed mentally ill ass, but it was hard for me to be a good partner. We fought, made up, fucked, fought again. Repeat. I didn't know it at the time but quite a few of her friends were encouraging her to dump me. Though she probably should have, we still stuck together. She cheered me up when I would come home sad and tired from work, where I often felt exploited and kicked around. And I was there for her when she would get homesick for Detroit.

During those years, Prince dropped three albums in quick succession. The first was *3121*, which took its title from the street address of the house Prince was renting out in Los Angeles from NBA player Carlos Boozer. It's said that Prince completely remodeled the house to meet his specifications, right on down to changing the carpet and painting the walls—and didn't even ask Boozer if it was okay. You have to admire that kind of chutzpah.

3121 is an album I sometimes overlook. It's a perfectly good album, full of funk and flavor, but few of the songs contained within are flat-out classics. It's got it moments, though. The single "Black Sweat" is dope as fuck, with Dr. Dre-like G-funk whistles paired with a retro-sounding drum machine. While admittedly sounding dated due to its early '90s West Coast rap-style production, it's still a monster of a jam. The track was nominated for a Grammy for Best R&B Song and Best Male R&B Vocal Performance and while it didn't win, it should have.

One of the other great singles from the album is "Te Amo Corazon," a slow, sexy, delicate love ballad, featuring a dope music video directed by Salma Hayek. I remember this was one of the last CD singles I ever bought.

This was a great time for Prince and it proved his comeback was no fluke. The album debuted at #1 on the Billboard charts—incredibly the first time that had ever happened—and it went Gold despite getting minimal airplay. Prince also entered the world of fragrance by coming out with a line of *3121* perfume products. It smelled like you would imagine Prince smelling—heavy base of lavender with notes of patchouli and vetiver. In true Prince fashion though, he didn't promote the scent much beyond one concert in Minneapolis, and the makers of the perfume ended up suing him for lack of promotion. Oh, that was our Prince.

A year later, the man dropped *Planet Earth*, which stands as my favorite album of this period. Now Prince was teamed up with a set of attractive identical twins – The Twinz – who danced furiously behind him as he performed. I remember seeing a Verizon commercial featuring the song "Guitar" in a movie theater. "Guitar" is loud, harsh, and full of funky Prince bravado about how his guitar will always be his one true love. I like this song. A lot. The other song on this album that I can't get enough of is "Mr. Goodnight," a laid back, silky smooth seduction number featuring Prince in full mack daddy mode. The song has him seducing a woman by telling her how he's going to treat her to the most perfect evening imaginable. He starts by telling her to go to a hotel room where she is to choose a dress to wear, then for her to call him and let him know which one she chose so he can wear a matching suit. Daaaaaamn. But he's not done yet. He invites his quarry to watch the movie "Chocolat" on a movie screen and then he purrs about wine, Moet, and Raisinets. Nobody could seduce a woman like Prince. No. Body.

Other favorites on *Planet Earth* includes the funky workout "Chelsea Rodgers," which I always wondered if it was based on a relative of Prince's—Rogers, Rodgers, get it? Featuring the return of the great Rosie Gaines, "Chelsea Rodgers" is a number about a model who kicks all kinds of ass, sort of a sequel in spirit to "Pussy Control." Prince actually won his last Grammy for the excellent song "Future Baby Mama," which was never even released as a single.

Then came one of the defining Prince career moments. Something so incredible that it made even people who didn't listen to Prince sit up and go "whoa!" February 4, 2007. The night Prince played the Super Bowl.

I can't remember anything about the game and I'll bet most other people can't either, but everyone will probably remember where they were sitting while they watched Prince perform at the Super Bowl Halftime Show. If there were any doubts that Prince wasn't back in a big way, they were squashed that night.

Sabrina and I were living in this great loft with hardwood floors in Downtown Toledo that used to be a speakeasy for the notorious Midwest organized crime unit, the Purple Gang. The place was super haunted; we used to hear footsteps going up and down the hallway and staircase at night. When I think back to those years, Prince's Super Bowl performance is probably the biggest highlight.

The Super Bowl was in Florida and it was pouring rain at the stadium. I remember waiting for the commercials to die down and for the halftime show to start when suddenly my cell phone rang. Fuck! Who was this?

"Hello?" I answered, audibly irritated.

"Hey, Webber, you getting ready to watch Prince?" It was my coworker Rene, who I didn't even realize had my number.

"Yes!" I almost shouted. Rene, obviously taken aback, just replied, "Ummmm, sorry. I just wanted to make sure you weren't going to miss it." I felt like an asshole, she was just trying to be nice.

"That's OK. I'll let you know what I think tomorrow."

"OK."

Click.

Back to waiting for Prince. The commercials still weren't over but it had been a few minutes and they had to be getting close to coming back to the broadcast. I was so excited I was shaking. First it was with anticipation, then it turned to rage…because my phone was ringing again.

"Hello?" I barked into the phone.

"Webber, are you getting ready to watch Prince?" This time it was yet another co-worker, Meredith. I bit my lip a little to calm myself down. I had no right to yell at people who were just checking in on me to make sure I wasn't missing history with my favorite artist.

"Yes, I'm so fucking excited," I said, right at the moment that the commercials ended and the broadcast resumed. "OK, it's on! Gotta go! Talk to you tomorrow!" Click.

This was it. As the skies thundered and rain continued to belt down onto the stadium, a snake of blue neon emerged from the darkness on the field to form the Prince symbol. I jumped into the center of the living room while Sabrina sat on the couch, chuckled, and shook her head at me lovingly. God bless that girl. She knew this was a huge deal to me.

"We will…we will …" Suddenly the thundering lyrics of Queen erupted throughout the stadium. It was being sung by a female voice, probably one of The Twinz. After about 30 seconds of boom-boom-clap, there was a huge explosion of fireworks from the stage and then the opening lyrics to "Let's Go Crazy."

Oh my God! It was him! Another burst of fireworks followed and … bam. Prince, clad in a peach shirt, a black do rag, and a baby blue suit, appeared on the stage, backed up by The Twinz. The stage was positively soaked from the rain, and yet the girls and Prince—all of whom were wearing high heels—were dancing on the wet, slick-looking surface as if nothing was out of the ordinary.

Prince was pure fire that night. He sang a tight medley of hits, both his and others, that added up to an incredible performance. From a snippet of "Proud Mary" to a song from the Foo Fighters (which he probably covered because Grohl and company were quite fond of covering "Darling Nikki" in concert) to his own hits like "Baby I'm A Star" and a spine-tingling version of "Purple Rain," which concluded with everyone in the stadium—and me at home—singing the "Oooh-hoo-hoo-hoo"s.

Today, Prince's Super Bowl performance is rated among the best halftime shows of all time, if not THE best. I felt triumphant. For years I had been talking the gospel of Prince to anyone who would listen, and suddenly Prince had proven to the entire world that I hadn't been talking out my ass for all these years. I felt like calling my old high school friend Chris and asking him "Now how about THAT?" The Prince Super Bowl show was simply the best live performance I'd ever seen televised. Hands down. If I had never been a Prince fan before then, I would have become one after that show.

"Wow! Just…wow." Sabrina chimed in from the couch. "I see why you like him so much."

I turned to her and smiled. Then I kissed her.

Prince & The Revolution
Why the 5'2" Singer Is the Biggest Male Feminist Rock Star of the Last 25 Years ... Kinda
Bitch magazine, Summer 2008

Dig if you will the picture—the United States, 1982. Ronald Reagan is in his second year as the president who will have waited until 21,000 Americans have died of AIDS before discussing it in a speech. The Equal Rights Amendment once again fails to be ratified, thanks in large part to Phyllis Schlafly and the religious right. A Gallup poll reveals that 51 percent of Americans find homosexuality immoral. And beamed onto television screens across this recession-plagued nation, from a fledgling cable channel known as MTV, a diminutive man sporting a purple trench-coat, mascara, heels, and the most lascivious smile this side of Rhett Butler gyrates on a soundstage, singing an innuendo-drenched song called "Little Red Corvette." His name is Prince, and he's come for your children.

Throughout the next two decades, he will fill their young, impressionable minds with lyrics that champion sexual and racial equality, androgyny, God, and the joys of masturbation. He will pen lyrics about the pain of incest ("Sister"), spin a rags-to-riches tale of a woman who triumphs over every man who gets in her way ("Pussy Control"), long openly to be a woman so as to better understand his lover ("If I Was Your Girlfriend"), and cry foul over the misogyny of gangsta rap ("Days of Wild"). He'll also star in a blatantly misogynistic box-office hit (1984's Purple Rain), write songs with titles like "Good Pussy" and "Irresistible Bitch," strut through the '80s and much of the '90s with a reputation as one of rockdom's most notorious playboys, and eventually become a Jehovah's Witness who refuses to swear in his lyrics or sing the songs that once made him the Moses of sexual freedom.

More so than any other popular male musician of the last three decades, the chart-topping artist known as Prince has extolled some of the strongest feminist and diversity-championing lyrics ever to come out of a speaker system. But considering how many times he's contradicted himself, is it possible that maybe he really was dreaming when he wrote them?

1980s: "am i black or white?/ am i straight or gay?"

If you joined the Columbia House Record and Tape Club in the early '80s, you would find that on the enroll-ment card under "Musical Interest," "Black music" had its own tidy category. But Prince's *Dirty Mind* album, a taut, 30-minute ode to sexual anarchy, greeted the Decade of Greed with an open invitation to everyone—gay, straight, man, woman, Black, white, whatever—to join a party where the only thing that mattered was how nasty you could get.

The precociously self-assured, barely-out-of-his-teens Prince kick-started the musical orgy with the song "Uptown," his vision of a sexual and racial utopia where it was "white, black, Puerto Rican/ Everybody just a-freakin.'" The number opens with Prince being stopped in the street by a woman who asks him "Are you gay?" Unmoved, he responds, "No, are you?" and boogies on, chalking the woman's attitude up to simple ignorance ("She's just a crazy, crazy, crazy little mixed-up dame/ She's just a victim of society and all its games"). Elsewhere on the album is "Head," a song that finds our hero receiving oral sex *from a bride on her way to the altar. But what could have been just another boastful, raunchy funk number about the joys of womanizing gets turned on its head when Prince returns the favor and promises to please his lady— who "married [him] instead"—with nonstop cunnilingus. Indeed, the majority of Prince's racy material focuses on the female orgasm, from early efforts like 1979's "I Wanna Be Your Lover" ("I wanna be the only one who makes you cum…running!") to his 1991 no. 1 hit "Cream" ("Cream/ Get on top/ Cream/ You will cop") to the obscure B-side "I Love U in Me" ("I promise myself not to cum until she does/ Then she took both hands/ And a liar I was").*

With the release of his next effort, 1981's Controversy, Prince perfected his manifesto. The title track dispensed with metaphor and got down to business, with Prince directly addressing the critics who found his material sala-cious and possibly dangerous to the youth of America. He concludes the title song with a rapped verse: "People call me rude/ I wish we were all nude/ I wish there was no black or white/ I wish there were no rules." The follow-ing track, "Sexuality," is a rallying cry for his brothers-and-sisters-in-arms to attack the oppressive moral and social norms around them ("Sexuality is all you'll ever need/ Sexuality/ Let your body be free"). And several years before the term "safe sex" ever passed the lips of a public health official, the album-losing boogie-woo-gie ditty "Jack U Off" found Prince offering to manually masturbate his date at the movies.

Prince's sexual persona was even more energized after the advent of MTV, when videos from his 1982 album 1999 kicked into heavy rotation. But even as the new medium of music video was making household names out of androgynous musicians like Grace Jones, Adam

Ant, and Annie Lennox, Prince (along with Jones and Michael Jackson, among the first black performers to appear on the channel) was a confounding spectacle for mainstream America—a sexually provocative man who danced in high-heeled suede boots in one video and was tied to a bed and whipped by two women in another. When he opened for the Rolling Stones in the early '80s, he was quickly booed offstage.

Clearly, this was a man ahead of his time. "The world wasn't ready for a performer like Prince," recalls Edna Gundersen, a rock critic for USA Today and a long-time Prince fan. "There had never been a performer so brazenly sexual, and even though some artists around that time were making heads turn, Prince was the first artist to really stand up and shout "Sex is good." He didn't treat sex as something to simply get attention with. And as a woman, I thought that was so liberating."

But then came 1984 and the release of Purple Rain. The movie's soundtrack still ranks high on many critics' lists of the best albums ever recorded. The film itself, though, took Prince's sex-freak persona to a darker, more sinister place than any of his previous music. The film, Prince's only box-office success, casts him as a struggling musician with an abusive father who has passed along his habit of hitting women to his son. Throughout the film, Morris Day and Jerome Benton (who fronted the Prince-formed R&B outfit The Time) refer to women as "bitches," and one notorious scene shows Benton picking up Day's scorned girlfriend and throwing her into a dumpster. Prince's character, The Kid, is equally prone to violence against women, in one scene punching his girlfriend (Apollonia) after she tells him she's joining Day's band.

The Kid was definitely a disturbing departure and left many of us worried that the pro-lady sex machine of "Uptown," "Head," and others was a ruse—especially since the film was billed as semiautobiographical. The film's vile treatment of women did not go unnoticed by critics. Leonard Maltin praised the film's concert sequences—some of the best ever filmed—but said "the film suffers from sexist, unappealing characters (especially Prince's)." Gundersen, who has interviewed the notoriously press-wary musician a few times over the years, agrees that Purple Rain's treatment of women is difficult to defend, but doesn't believe that the character of The Kid is an accurate representation of Prince. "He contradicts himself on occasion, as we all do. But [Prince] has a great deal of respect for women. He's always taken female sexuality very seriously, and that's rare for a male artist."

For some, in fact, Prince apparently took female sexuality a bit too seriously. Tipper Gore, for one, was inspired to found the watchdog group Parents Music Resource Center after walking by her 8-year-old daughter's room and hearing "Darling Nikki," in which Prince sings of the title character, "I met her in a hotel lobby/ Masturbating with a magazine." *Purple Rain, which was perched atop Billboard's album charts for a stunning 23 weeks, was soon being dissected and analyzed—from cover art to lyrics—by members of a shocked and apalled Congress. The record industry soon adopted the now-common-place Parental Advisory sticker in response to albums like Purple Rain, as well as those by contemporaries like Twisted Sister, Mötley Crüe, and Wendy O. Williams.*

But parental-advisory warnings notwithstanding, Prince continued to complicate the way sexuality and gender were dealt with in mainstream music. His magnum opus had to be "If I Was Your Girlfriend," from 1987's Sign O' The Times. Twenty years later, it remains one of the most genderfuck songs ever recorded. The vocals on the track are credited to an alter ego, "Camille," and his voice is sped up to a high-pitched tone that sounds neither male nor female but alien. Predictably, it flopped as a single. America may have tolerated Prince's high-heeled boots and bikini briefs, but it wasn't going to stomach a song in which a man ponders what it would be like to be his lover's female friend so that he could truly know her deepest thoughts and feelings ("If I was your girlfriend/ Would you remember/ To tell me all the things you forgot when I was your man?").

As Liz Jones wrote in her Prince biography, Purple Reign, "[Prince] invites men to imagine a different way of relating to women and invites women to imagine men who could imagine such things." When you consider that 1987 was the same year gangsta-rap pioneers N.W.A. released their debut album, which featured songs like "A Bitch Iz a Bitch" and introduced suburban kids to terms like "ho" and "skank," such imagination seems rare indeed.

1990s: "a woman everyday should be thanked/ not disrespected, not raped or spanked"

In 1991, nine years after he first strutted across MTV screens, Prince was back on the channel, this time dressed in a buttocks-baring banana-yellow suit. His performance of the sultry jam "Gett Off" at the 1991 MTV Video Awards was undeniably one of his best live efforts; even the numerous jokes about the buttless pants couldn't over-shadow the power of the performance.

The 1990s will forever be remembered as the decade hip hop broke through to become a full-blown cultural force and one of the dominant musical mediums, and our mascaraed dandy couldn't compete with the aggression of Tupac Shakur and Dr. Dre. Prince, who had never been comfortable with rap, and once even wrote a song parodying it ("Dead On It"), suddenly found himself looking dangerously old hat. No matter how shocking a lyric like "I sincerely wanna fuck the taste out of your mouth" had been in 1982, it was no match for the in-your-face rhymes offered by the Notorious B.I.G., Eazy-E, or Too $hort ("She's like another girl named Christina/ Bitch so dumb, I named her 'misdemeanor'").

Prince's 1991 album Diamonds and Pearls—considered by many critics to be his "sellout" album, with its unabashed appropriation of hip hop—would be his last bona fide smash album of the millennium. Like many '80s megastars, Prince was quickly demoted to he-was-cool-once-upon-a-time status, and his '90s output was earmarked by two crucial events—his marriage to former bandmate Mayte Garcia and his struggle to free himself from his contract with Warner Bros. Records. The effort to draw attention to the money-over-creativity workings of major labels was well in line with Prince's provocateur character; unfortunately, spending the mid-'90s with the word "slave" scrawled on his cheek at public appearances, and changing his name to an unpronounceable symbol, led mostly to his becoming a punch line for late-night talk-show hosts.

But slumping record sales didn't stop Prince from continuing to pen songs like "Pussy Control," a you-go-girl anthem starring an impoverished, bullied girl who rises to attain wealth and success, all the while ignoring the advances of pick-up artists and trifling players ("Pussy got bank in her pockets/ Before she got dick in her drawers/ If a brother didn't have good and plenty of his own/ In love, Pussy never did fall"). One of his top hits of the '90s, "The Most Beautiful Girl in the World," reassured women that, contrary to the rigid physical beauty standards imposed upon them, true beauty comes from within ("'Cause honey, this kind of beauty has got no reason to ever be shy/ 'Cause honey, this kind of beauty is the kind that comes from inside"). Corny? Absolutely. But for 1994— where Prince found himself having more in common, attitude-wise, with Riot Grrrl bands like Bikini Kill than with the average mainstream male singer—his ballad stood out.

Though Prince's '90s albums were consistently greeted with mixed reviews, they reflect a growing maturity in his approach to life, women, and relationships. During his long banishment to the pop culture wilderness, Prince was still challenging sexual and gender roles, albeit on a less obvious scale. In a 1996 interview with Oprah Winfrey, he candidly discussed his name change to "the symbol," which was a fusion of the male and female biological signs. Prince (who Oprah said "looked pretty") told his host that, through therapy, he had discovered that he had another person inside him, saying, "And I haven't discovered what sex that person is yet."

Following 1996's Emancipation, Prince rarely returned to the smolderingly sexual material that once made him Public Enemy No. 1 in the eyes of parents and hand-wringing conservatives. But remaining ahead of his time in some ways couldn't stop Prince for falling behind it in others. Genuinely aghast at the culture of contemporary music, Prince's stomping, raucous funk number "Days of Wild"—from 1997's self-released Crystal Ball—lashed out

*at the entertainment industry with salvos aimed specifi-
cally at the rampant misogyny of hip hop ("Hooker, bitch
and ho?/ I don't think so/ I only knew one and never told
her though/ I thought about it many times/ But that's the
kinda shit to make you check your mind"). The song ends
with a heartfelt shout-out to women: "Much props to the...
baddest, freezer-burnin', head-turnin', make-a-brother-
yearnin' sistas (who are) walkin' the face/ You know who
you are."*

*Prince ended the '90s on a fascinating note. His 1999
album Rave Un2 the Joy Fantastic, though yet another
commercial flop, shows the notorious control freak collab-
orating with tough female artists like Gwen Stefani ("So
Far, So Pleased"), Eve ("Undisputed"), and Ani Difranco ("I
Love U But I Don't Trust U Anymore"). It's hard to imagine
any of these women taking shit from any man.*

*Yet this is precisely what makes Prince such a frus-
tratingly contradictory artist. His love for working with
strong women aside, Prince has often toed a thin line
between championing female sexual empowerment and
expounding garden-variety sexism. Alex Hahn's dishy bio
Possessed: The Rise and Fall of Prince paints him as domineering in relationships (he reputedly made ex-flame
Carmen Electra "be immaculately dressed and groomed,
even while doing errands") and strongly judgmental, at
one point telling ex-bandmates and romantic couple
Wendy Melvoin and Lisa Coleman, "You're gonna burn
in hell for your lifestyle!"*

*And what are we to make of the songs he wrote for
female artists like Sheena Easton, who scored one of her
biggest hits with the Prince-penned "Sugar Walls"? Easton
purrs her way through lyrics like "Come spend the night
inside my sugar walls" and "Take advantage, it's alright/*

*Your body's on fire, admit it/ Come inside." Is Easton a
sexually liberated woman or a projection of Prince's fanta-
sies? And then there was the Prince-created girl group
Vanity 6, a trio of lingerie-clad vamps who cooed songs
like "Nasty Girl" and "Vibrator." Prince originally wanted
to call the group The Hookers, and before he christened
group member Denise Mathews "Vanity," he suggested
her stage name be "Vagina."*

*Who was this mysterious person who could acknowl-
edge a female presence inside him and even give it a
name, who could make women the center of his world
one minute and then reduce them to their genitalia the
next? It seemed, throughout the '80s and '90s, that Prince
himself may never have been sure—but his next move was
one that no one expected.*

2000 and beyond: "no, i ain't dead yet/ but what about you?"

*In November 2001, Prince dropped a jazzy, complex,
and commercially ignored album called The Rainbow
Children. There was no swearing. No appearances from
his Camille persona. None of the "salvation through sex"
anthems that once helped him amass a racially and sexually diverse fan base of millions who believed, like him,
that "making love and music are the only things worth
fighting for." (Or who just liked the music.)*

*Instead, The Rainbow Children, a concept album
packed with allusions to Prince's newly adopted Jehovah's
Witness faith—a notoriously conservative, patriarchal
sect of Christianity—included a song called "Muse 2 the
Pharaoh," which contained the lyric "There is nothing he
wouldn't give her, see/ For the future of the nation rests
in her belly/ And if the Proverbs of the 31 and verse 10/*

Becomes the verse she sings again and again/ She might be Queen." Behold the King James Version of Proverbs 31:10 –"Who can find a virtuous woman? For her price is far above rubies."

Clearly, this was not your older brother's Prince.

Thankfully, Prince's subsequent albums mostly refrained from such obvious patriarchal preachiness, but while his recent output doesn't negate his earlier pro-feminist/pro-freak material, it's apparent that Prince has moved far out of the Uptown neighborhood of sexual and social nonconformity that he once sang about. But then again, don't all artists usually mellow out at some point, leaving it to the young acolytes they influenced to carry on the tradition of keeping parents angry and the masses riled?

The Madonna who created the Sex book, embarked on "The Girlie Show" tour, and fellated Evian bottles has been replaced by a sophisticated mother of two who now cuts entertaining, but certainly more innocuous, albums. Famed '70s hellraiser Rod Stewart has reinvented himself as a neo-crooner, singing inoffensive songs from the '40s and '50s to stadiums full of retirees. Even human peacock Elton John, who once co-wrote songs about drugged-up young lesbians ("All the Girls Love Alice") and cruising ("Big Dipper"), now finds himself writing songs for children's movies. The difference, perhaps, is that none of these artists condemn their former work in their current output.

The last few years have seen Prince's fortunes change once again. Following a jaw-dropping duet with Beyoncé at the 2004 Grammy Awards and his admission to the Rock and Roll Hall of Fame, Prince returned to the top of the charts for the first time since the early '90s, with the albums *Musicology* and *3121*. His older fans have mostly forgotten that they used to ridicule him for the symbol name or the assless pants, and instead remember him for his stunning 2007 Super Bowl halftime show, his residency concerts in Las Vegas, or one of his many sold-out tours; the younger fans just like the music.

Surveying his long, contradictory career, it's not hard to argue that Prince is the most complicated and confounding male artist of the modern rock era—a man who played and toyed with sex, gender, and race like few others ever have. Looking through a feminist lens at Prince's canon of work reveals a complicated kaleidoscope of potentially empowering songs with messages of sexual and social equality, mixed in with the occasional sidestep into standard-issue pop-music sexism.

To be sure, he'll never be canonized as a feminist saint; it's tough to get around songs with titles like "Scarlet Pussy" and "Billy Jack Bitch." But in a male-dominated rock world known for celebrating machismo at its basest level, Prince still stands apart from the pack. Whatever his missteps, dearly beloved, Prince's sexual-spiritual belief that men and women are more alike than different is something that few other male artists have expressed with such ardor or style—that sexy MF.

(Reprinted by permission)

XI.

*B*y 2008, I was tired, and frustrated. I'd been working at Toledo City Paper for more than four years and had lost most of my enthusiasm for community journalism. The ratio of salary to stress level just didn't make sense, and I figured I needed to try something new with my journalism degree, which was becoming more useless with every passing year.

After sending out résumés for marketing and public relations positions all over the country and coming up empty, I dropped off an application package on the doorstep of Toledo Mayor Carty Finkbeiner. The mayor had publicly stated that if there was a young person in Toledo who was thinking about leaving the city due to being unable to find a job, they could send him their résumé and he would help them find a position. I didn't know if the mayor was trying to make himself look good or if he was sincere, but I took him up on his offer.

I dropped off a letter explaining my background and included a few of my writing samples. Two days later I got a call from his office that the mayor wanted to see me.

When I went to his office, Mayor Finkbeiner was friendly and gracious, which was in stark contrast to his reputation. He was known for being an intense rageaholic and was once sued by a City of Toledo employee when he allegedly threw a coffee cup at her head. And that was just one of the many stories about Carty. In fact,

Finkbeiner was such a character that the local daily newspaper even published a book called *The Little Book of Carty*, which collected various anecdotes about his colorful behavior.

I knew Finkbeiner a little; I'd interviewed him for Toledo City Paper a few times over the years. After exchanging pleasantries, he asked what kind of job I was looking for. I told him something in the public relations sector. Then he hit the speaker on his phone and punched in an extension.

"Hey, Bob?"

"Yes, Mayor?" a soft voice answered.

"Listen, I have a young man here in my office that I think might be an asset to our team," Finkbeiner said into the phone. "I'm going to give you his résumé and I want you to take a look at it."

"Sure, no problem," Bob answered on the other end.

Wait a minute. "Asset to our team?" I didn't want a job in government, especially one working for Mayor Carty Finkbeiner. I'd heard the stories and I didn't want to work for someone who screamed all the time. I'd endured enough of that growing up.

But wait a minute. If I worked for Carty, that would look incredible on a résumé. So the guy was a yeller; so was my old man. I decided right then and there that I wanted to work for Finkbeiner. It was just too good of an opportunity to pass up.

About a month later, Finkbeiner called me in to tell me "we want to take you on board," a decision that promptly met with controversy on the Toledo City Council because the city was awash in red ink and it was considered excessive to hire any new people at a time when the city should have been cutting back.

I was a bit shaken by the fact that I was suddenly being talked about on the news, but I swallowed my concern. I had a great new job making nine thousand dollars more than I had working at Toledo City Paper. What could go wrong?

Everything.

I ended the first day on the job as the Public Information Officer—ie: Carty's spokesperson—sobbing in the arms of Ms. Gabriel, one of his chiefs of staff. Carty had unleashed a torrent of rage at me on his way out the door, wondering why I didn't have a speech complete for a press conference that was three days away. When I reminded him that the press conference wasn't for a few days, that only made him scream louder.

"I expect excellence!" he roared in my face, flecks of spittle bulleting my cheeks. "I don't care if you're the new guy. This is how it's done around here!" He then stormed off and out the door and I went into my office, put my head on the desk and burst into tears.

I knew what to expect. I'd heard all the stories. I thought I'd prepared myself for everything. But nothing had braced me for the harsh reality of dealing with Carty's moods.

I wiped my eyes, got up, and made a beeline for the men's room so I could wash my face and pull myself together. But I passed Ms. Gabriel along the way and she could tell I was upset.

"You okay? What's the matter?" asked Ms. Gabriel.

Still a mess, I looked into her face and promptly burst into tears again, sobbing so hard I couldn't' speak. She pulled me into a hug. "C'mere, baby."

I had never been spoken to like that before. Even at his maddest, Dad had never roared in my face like that. I was shaken to my very core and also extremely embarrassed to be crying my first day on the job out in the open of the main office of One Government Center.

Ms. Gabriel let me go and held me by my shoulders, looking into my tear-streaked eyes. "I'm going to tell you straight. You need to toughen up. He's a screamer. I don't like it, nobody likes it. But it's the way he is. You can't take it personally."

I nodded that I understood. And I did. I thanked Ms. Gabriel, went into the men's room and splashed cold water on my red face.

After quickly checking for feet under the toilet stall, I gave myself a pep talk in the mirror.

"Shut up! Just shut up! You gonna start crying like a bitch because someone gets in your face? Man up, for God's sake! Man the fuck up!"

The next day I went into work, determined to not let myself lose my cool or composure ever again. Ice cold, Webber, ice cold, I told myself silently.

As I sat at my desk, Carty popped his head into my office doorway. "Hey, Jase, how you doing, partner?"

"Oh, um, hi, Mayor," I stammered, feeling my hands beginning to shake a little.

"I just wanted to say 'good morning.' Talk to you soon." With that, he left.

And that was Carty– a berserker rage one minute, lucid and friendly the next.

For the next nine months, my reality was a nightmare. Carty would call me at all hours of the night to yell for a myriad of reasons, from supposed errors I'd made in his speeches, to find out why so-and-so in the water department did something. After about a month, if my phone would ring after 6 p.m., I had a Pavlovian response and go into a panic attack. My doctor, not knowing at the time this would be a regrettable decision, prescribed me Xanax as a way of dealing with the anxiety and the panic attacks. The Xanax certainly helped but I quickly came to rely on them as a crutch against the stress of Carty and I started taking far more than I was prescribed. It was my first encounter with the little demons.

In 2008, Facebook was still relatively in its infancy and MySpace was the dominant social network. I updated my MySpace every day and spent much of my free time goofing off on the platform. But I also kept a journal going about my life. All of my MySpace friends were people that I knew, so I felt comfortable being candid and letting it all hang out, so to speak. So I blogged about what working for Carty was like. I compared him to Yosemite Sam for his tendency to yell. I also shared that working for Carty was "soul-crushing" and "surreal" and that I felt like I was starring "in a low-rent version of 'The Devil Wears Prada.'"

Besides blogging, the main thing that got me through the Carty period was the fact that Prince had released two albums at the same time. One of the mayor's administrative professionals, Lesa, was a huge Prince fan and we both got the albums on the same day and it was fun to compare our favorite tracks. It was a great mood booster to suddenly have new music from Prince in the middle of one of the darkest periods of my life.

The two albums, *Lotusflo3er* and *MPLSound*, were wonderfully retro, especially *MPLSound*, which sounded like it was lifted directly from 1982. This was an album that could shut up the naysayers who wished Prince would go back to "the old school." Prince uses vintage drum machines on this record, and the title indicates he's intentionally going for that classic "Minneapolis sound." The opening track "(There'll Never B) Another Like Me" is a fun, funky romp of Prince just sounding like he's having a good time. In fact, the whole album has a party-out-of-bounds feeling to it. But unlike the empty-souled, phoned-in funk of *Newpower Soul*, *MPLSound* feels like Prince is really into it and is enjoying giving the people what they want—vintage-sounding, classic Prince funk. The song "Better With Time" is a love song to Prince's former "Under the Cherry Moon" co-star Kristen Scott-Thomas, while "Valentina" is addressed to Salma Hayek's little girl, who Prince beseeches to tell her famous mama to give him a call after she's done chasing the kid around the house. Prince hasn't sounded this happy in years and *MPLSound* is a great time.

Lotusflo3wer is the lesser of the two albums, but it still has a few great moments, particularly Prince's amazing cover of "Crimson and Clover," which he performed on Ellen Degeneres' show. The album is Prince's most hippy-dippy sounding work since *Around the World In A Day*, with dreamy, swirly psychedelia dominating most of the songs. It's cool hearing Prince back in touch with his peace/love side, even if the album as a whole is mostly average.

As I reveled in new Prince music, I had no idea that things were about to get really interesting. One March morning, I got a call from a reporter at a weekly newspaper who started asking me "Are these your blog entries on Swamp Things?" Swamp Things was a local website operated by a guy named Carl Driscoll who was a local political wannabe. Every year, he ran for school board and always came in last place. The guy was mostly considered a joke.

"What blog entries?" I asked, while typing 'Swamp things' into the Google search engine.

"Ummmm, you call Carty 'Yosemite Sam' and, ummm, you say he's digging his political grave," said the reporter, who was obviously young and inexperienced. As Swamp Things loaded, I suddenly remembered the blog entries I'd written on MySpace months ago. Wait a second. Those several month-old blog entries, which was basically just me having a laugh, were on my private blog, which was only available to my MySpace friends. And Carl Driscoll was definitely not on my friend's list.

There it was. The headline read "How can the Mayor's spokesperson do his job if he thinks the mayor is 'digging his political grave'?" The blog entries were all right there. My mouth went instantly dry.

"Yes. Those are my blog entries," I managed to croak.

"Ok. Do you have any comment about these blog entries being posted?"

I was starting to get literally dizzy. "No." I hung up the phone.

I sat there and just stared at the screen with questions flashing through my brain. What…how…who…where? I couldn't focus. All I could do was stare at the monitor with my mouth agape. This was very, very, very bad.

And then the phone rang again. It was Lloyd Madison, one of the local television anchors.

"Hi, Jason, how you doing? It's Lloyd Madison."

"Ummmm…yeah…ummmm…I'm not really doing that well, Lloyd" I stammered into the phone. "I have no idea where he got those."

"I'm sorry, Jason. You know we have to do a story on this, right?"

"Yeah, I understand that, Lloyd. I…" I trailed off. There was nothing to say. This was now a news story whether I liked it or not. I noted the irony of the fact that as Carty's spokesperson, I was responsible for getting him in the media. Now suddenly, I personally was the topic of discussion. This wasn't supposed to happen.

Soon the entire city was buzzing about what I'd written about Carty. Bloggers all over Toledo were weighing in on the situation. Most people basically wanted to crack me and Driscoll's heads together—Driscoll for violating the terms of a private blog and me for being stupid enough to put my personal feelings about Carty onto the internet. And it was stupid. No question.

I stayed in my office and waited. I knew what was coming. It was time to face the music. At around 2 p.m. that day, Carty came to my office and shut the door behind him without saying a word.

I stood up and walked to the center of the room. Carty, his face a red mask of rage, slowly walked up to me and put his face next to mine, looking right into my eyes.

"I oughta fucking spit right in your face," he growled, in a low, raspy voice.

"The door's closed, Mayor. Do what you gotta do," I replied, not knowing what else I could say or do.

"You listen to me, young man. You did something really, really stupid and you're going to pay the price."

"I understand, Mayor," I said, trying to act how James Bond would if he were getting grilled by M, his boss. I stood perfectly still, looking Carty in the face and not letting my gaze break.

We stared at each other like that for a minute. Then Carty looked away and walked out the door, slamming it behind him.

I sat down at my computer and brought up a fresh Word document.

I hereby announce my resignation from the City of Toledo, effective immediately.

Thank You,

Jason Webber

I printed out the letter on City of Toledo letterhead and signed it. I then opened my office door, making eye contact with Lesa and Barbara, the Mayor's secretaries, who didn't say anything. They just looked at me with sympathy. I dropped the letter off in the Mayor's mailbox, and went back to my office.

I had a few voicemails on my cell phone from friends and colleagues, all asking if I was alright. I appreciated the support but couldn't bring myself to call anyone back. I stood there in my office, looking out the window at the city of Toledo and for a moment, hurling myself through the glass and plummeting to the asphalt below flashed before my mind. Though this had some allure, I knew I wasn't really ready to splatter myself all over the sidewalk for the likes of Carty Finkbeiner.

But at that moment, as I saw my career slipping away towards a completely unknown future, I asked myself "What would Prince do?"

Prince was known for being really tough to work for. There had been dozens of interviews with engineers, producers, and ex-bandmates, all of whom had testified that Prince could be a monster at times. As I stood there in my office, I imagined myself having a conversation with Prince about this situation I found myself in.

So I fucked up, Prince. I let my ass overload my brain, as my old man might say, and I embarrassed myself and my boss. If you were my boss, you'd fire my ass, wouldn't you?

Not necessarily. Did U learn something from this experience?

Yes, I certainly did. I learned that I'm reckless with the internet and I need to learn to keep my mouth shut.

OK. U learned something. R U going 2 do anything like this again?

No. No way.

So no, I wouldn't fire U. You've learned a valuable lesson here.

I was woken out of my imaginary conversation with Prince by my cell phone buzzing in my pocket. I took it out to see who it was and it was Jerry Cusack, one of the Mayor's many advisors. Why would he be calling?

"Hello?" I asked, my voice quaking.

"Hey, Jase, how you holding up?" said Jerry, concern evident in his voice.

"To be honest, not very well, Jerry. I embarrassed the mayor and I embarrassed myself. I don't know how I'm going to get out of this one."

"Well, I spoke to Carty and I've advised him to go easy on you. What you did was stupid, no doubt about that, but I don't think you're a bad guy."

Hearing this from Jerry made tears burn my eyes.

"I certainly feel like a bad guy, Jerry. I was so reckless, I didn't even think something like this could happen."

"Well, you've learned a lesson then, haven't you?"

"And how."

"Well, just hang in there," said Jerry. "This too shall pass." I hated that cliché but I was so happy to hear it at that moment.

"Thanks, Jerry, I really appreciate you calling," I said into the receiver.

"Hang in there, Jason. You're a good man."

"Thanks, Jerry. Take care."

"You too."

Jerry and I hung up and I wiped away the hot tears that were running down my face. Jerry and my imaginary friend version of Prince were right: I had indeed learned a lesson, probably something that was already obvious to most people but all I can say is: You try working in politics some time. It's a crazy world unto itself.

That night I went home and crashed after putting away the best part of a bottle of Jack Daniels. I felt I'd hit bottom. Sabrina, who I'd split with right around the time I started working for Carty, came over and just held my pathetic drunk ass as I sobbed. My career was probably over, so I might as well drink my sorrows away. Even as inebriated as I got, I still showed up for work dutifully at 8 a.m. After all, the Mayor hadn't said I was fired or not even though I had tendered my resignation.

The next day, the Mayor was due to give a speech to the Toledo Press Club. I showed up, loaded up the podium, prepared his remarks just as I always had. The Mayor didn't converse with me during our brief interactions and I didn't have the balls to ask him about the letter of resignation I'd turned in.

Then after his speech, the Mayor suddenly started talking about me to the members of the press that had come to watch him speak.

"I know there has been a lot of discussion this week about the City of Toledo's public information officer. I'm here to announce that he will be keeping his position. Jason Webber is a good man, but inexperienced. I'm confident that he has learned a valuable lesson and we're going to move forward from here."

My throat constricted as I heard the Mayor speak those words. After all this, I wasn't being fired? I felt like going to church and kneeling at the altar, exclaiming "Thank you! Thank you!"

That night on the news, I was once again the number one topic. The media acted surprised I was keeping my job, but really, I wasn't. By keeping me on board, Carty appeared regal and kind, a strong counterbalance to his usual press. From a PR perspective, keeping me on board was a shrewd, if cynical, move. But all I knew is I wasn't fired.

At least not then. Two months later, I, along with 70 other people at the City of Toledo were let go as a way to save costs. That day I packed a box up with my belongings and left my government job, listening to Dolly Parton's "Hard Candy Christmas" on repeat as I drove away in my hooptie Kia Rio.

When I got home, I once again closed my eyes and wondered what Prince would say if he was here.

Well, did U learn a lot during U're time with the city?

Yeah, I sure did.

Then it was a success. Move on. Grab the next brass ring that comes around.

What if one doesn't come around again?

Then U go looking for 1.

The brass ring DID come up again, in a way I hadn't expected: Working for Insane Clown Posse.

XII.

$\mathcal{I}$'m a Juggalo. I love the Insane Clown Posse. Sorry, not sorry. Besides Prince and David Bowie, the most important musical element in my life has been Violent J and Shaggy 2 Dope and the whole Dark Carnival mythos. I've been down with the Clown since 1997, when my friend Rick at Just Music played me some snippets from *The Great Milenko*. I was hooked from the first time I heard "Hokus Pokus" and "Chicken Huntin' (Slaughterhouse Mix)." In the late '90s, if you would've told me I'd grow up to work for my favorite rap group, I would've laughed and said you were more insane than the two greasepainted harlequins from the streets of Detroit.

But life has a funny way of taking you into directions you never imagined.

After I got laid off by Carty, I found a job working for another mayor, this time down in Dayton. In early July of 2009, I went to Dayton on a blind date to meet a girl named Melissa who responded to my Plenty of Fish dating profile. We had a lot of cool, weird shit in common. We each loved Andrew W.K., shared a mutual love of absinthe, and we both had grown up being social outcasts in small towns. On our first date, we went to a Celtic festival in downtown Dayton, holding hands, and doing the "getting to know you" dance. Melissa was the kind of woman Leonard Cohen sang about in "Suzanne." She wore thrift store clothes, a well-loved pair of Doc Martens, and lots of bracelets and necklaces. She had big expressive eyes that made her look like a 1940s ingenue. She was absolutely gorgeous, smart, and funny as hell.

While we were meandering around, I saw a woman handing out leaflets for a mayoral candidate named Gary Leitzell. He was an independent who was running against the incumbent. I didn't know a thing about Dayton politics, but having worked for Carty, I knew a thing or two about working in government. As I was still unemployed at the time and my heart was aflutter with the pangs of infatuation with this awesome girl in Dayton, I suddenly found myself making small talk with the woman, who turned out to be Gary's wife.

I had an idea: What if I volunteered to be Gary's spokesperson and public relations guy during his campaign? If he loses, fine, no big deal; I'll just ask him to write me a letter of recommendation on campaign stationary. But what if he wins? I could move down to Dayton and I'd have a new city at my disposal, a new job, and maybe a new girlfriend. It was just the fresh start I needed.

And I'll be damned if it didn't work exactly out that way.

Gary won the election, I got hired as his personal aide, and Melissa and I fell in love. I guess some things are just meant to be. Never let anyone tell you serendipity and kismet don't exist.

I moved down to Dayton in January of 2010, right after Gary took the office of Mayor for the City of Dayton. It was a good job, but kind of tough because I had to get used to working for a City Manager form of local government, which was the exact opposite of the strong mayor form of government operated by Carty. In Dayton, the mayor was simply a member of the City Commission, one vote of four. Gary stood in stark contrast to everything about Carty, which still haunted me every day; I would later be diagnosed with post-traumatic stress disorder resulting from the year I'd spent with the Toledo mayor. Where Carty was a rageaholic and abusive, Gary was soft-spoken, humble, and an all-around pleasant person. He never considered himself a "politician," but "a problem solver." Even though his personal political stance ran to the right of mine, Gary was my kind of independent: Unpretentious, honest, and not totally driven by ego. After the megalomania of the Finkbeiner administration, working for Gary felt like a paid vacation. I worked in the City Commission office, and I'd go home to Melissa's house, which she shared with her awesome mom Pam, her brother Jordan and his girlfriend Megan. Melissa and I had the basement to ourselves and it started out as a cute little love nest between us, a marathon of so-bad-they're-good movies, good sex, and fun, goofy conversations.

Unfortunately, I once again screwed everything up. As 2010 went by, I was feeling really homesick for Toledo and Detroit. All of my friends were up there and the only mates I was making for myself in Dayton were people Melissa knew. I felt like a tagalong. Plus, I quickly fell into my bad cohabitational habit of needing excess space and spending too much time in my own head ruminating and dwelling on everything that was wrong with my life. This resulted in me being a moody bastard much of the time, and Melissa and I drifted apart slowly throughout the year.

December of 2010 was one of the worst months of my life. I knew Melissa had fallen out of love with me at that point, and I had a strong, panicky suspicion that she was developing feelings for one of her coworkers. I'd been sick with back-to-back ear and sinus infections for two months straight—part of the perils of living in a germ cesspool like the Miami Valley—and I was generally feeling like I was just spinning my wheels in Dayton. Where was the adventure I craved?

On December 12, I broke up with Melissa over mediocre burritos at a franchised faux-Mexican eatery. It was no great surprise to either of us, but I was seriously pissed at myself. I'd allowed yet another once decent relationship to fall apart. Two days after we split, Melissa did indeed start dating her coworker. Anxious to hurry up and get moved out, I ended up staying with a sympathetic family who let me crash on their basement couch while I tried to find an apartment. Not exactly a merry Christmas.

Two months later, I heard through a friend that Melissa eloped to Vegas and married her coworker.

Heartbroken, angry, and filled with jealousy and regret, I threw myself into writing as a way to combat the hurt. I started writing a column about the single life for the local alternative newsweekly, and through a Facebook connection, I started interviewing celebrities for VICE magazine, which at the time was the best writing gig I'd ever had. I interviewed Jack Black and Kyle Gass of Tenacious D, Jerky Boys creator Johnny Brennan, and filmmaker Jennifer Lynch, director of one of my favorite movies "Boxing Helena."

I also started writing an ambitious would-be cover story for the Metro Times in Detroit. My subject was the first white rapper to make any noise in the Motor City, an eccentric genius named Danny KAE (his surname is an acronym for 'K. Always excelling.). I'd heard about Danny through Violent J's excellent memoir about ICP "Behind the Paint." Danny's music was described as some of the worst rap you'd ever hear, but you couldn't help but fall in love with the guy because he was so sincere. Violent J and Shaggy 2 Dope were hugely influenced by Danny KAE, as were Kid Rock, Eminem, Uncle Kracker, and basically every other Caucasian rapper that came out of Detroit during the '90s.

While I was interviewing Shaggy 2 Dope of ICP for VICE, I also mentioned I was working on a feature-length profile on Danny KAE. Shaggy got excited and cheerfully answered several questions about Danny's influence and put me on the phone with Violent J to give his side of the interview. We ended up talking for about an hour and when I got off the phone, I felt elated. Both Violent J and Shaggy had spoken to me like I was a friend and not just some fanboy.

I had a memorable encounter—if you want to call what happened an 'encounter'— with Eminem while writing the Danny KAE piece. Eminem was known to be a fan of Danny's and I reached out to his manager Paul Rosenberg to see if Em would give me an interview. Paul got got back to me a few days later via email and said Eminem would provide a quote for the article, but first he needed to hear Danny KAE's albums again because it had been quite a few years since he'd heard them.

Excited, I called Danny in Alaska where he was living and told him to send me his CD catalog so I could get them to Eminem. Danny, an odd duck to the end, simply replied, "Well, who's going to pay for these CDs, Jason?" I was confused. "Danny, this is Eminem we're talking about. If we get a quote from him for the story, it's going to help us reach a whole new readership that we wouldn't get otherwise! C'mon! Just gimme the CDs." Danny wouldn't budge. "You have to pay for them." So I sent Danny $80 for his four albums and after a few weeks, I finally got them sent to Shady Records, Eminem's label. About a week later, I got an email from Paul with the quote from Eminem, which ended up being only one sentence. No matter. I had an original Eminem quote in my article. That was undeniably cool.

As I researched the Danny KAE story, I developed a solid friendship with a Detroit rapper named Champtown, an associate of Danny's and a rap legend in his own right. Champtown took Eminem to his very first professional studio recording back in 1992—to Paisley Park, no less. It turned out Champtown and Prince went way back, with Prince even playfully dissing Champtown on the song "Daddy Pop" from *Diamonds and Pearls*. During the early '90s, Champtown wore a jester's hat whenever he performed, and on "Daddy Pop" you can hear Rosie Gaines telling Prince, "It's the jester!" while Prince snarkily replies to "Tell him I'm not here!"

Champtown ended up becoming an important friend and professional colleague to me. After the Danny KAE story came out in July 2012, Champtown flew me to Minneapolis to put together a press kit for an up-and-coming rapper he was working with named Verdict, a nice kid with a lot of talent.

I was in Minni-fucking-apolis! I couldn't believe it! I wondered if I'd get a chance to see Prince? After spending the day hanging out at the studio Champtown, myself, Verdict, and Verdict's manager Pauly drove around Minneapolis, with Champtown showing me the sights. We drove past the legendary First Avenue, the Whiskey A-Go Go of the Midwest, where the bulk of "Purple Rain" took place.

We were super busy for the long weekend we were there in Minneapolis, but Champtown found the time to introduce me to some of his colleagues, including a visit with Walter Chancellor, an amazing saxophonist who played on *Emancipation* and Chaka Khan's Prince-produced album *Come 2 My House*. Walt was full of great stories about Prince and I even got to appear as background noise on one of his songs called "Smack It On the What."

I got totally starstruck when Champtown introduced me to St. Paul Peterson, the former lead singer of The Family, a side project Prince put together in the mid-'80s. The Family didn't last very long; Paul supposedly got fed up with not having any creative input, a common refrain among Prince proteges. The Family is best remembered for recording the initial version of the Prince composition "Nothing Compares 2 U," which Sinead O'Connor famously took to the top of the charts in 1990.

As we left the music school where Paul taught, and where Champtown had been a former faculty member, Champtown asked me if I wanted to go to Paisley Park.

"Fuck yeah!" I exclaimed. I couldn't believe it. I was going to get to see Paisley Park.

We drove about a half hour outside of Minneapolis to a suburb called Chanhassen and after taking a few twists and turns, Champtown pulled us up next to Paisley Park, a large white boxy complex that looked like something out of a '70s science fiction movie. The parking lot was gated and bolted and there were no cars to be seen. Clearly Prince was not home.

Champtown walked up to the large rolling gate and I followed him. He clearly knew what he was doing. In the blink of an eye, he grabbed one of the gate doors and pried it back, motioning me through.

"C'mon, Webb, hurry up," Champtown prodded as I slithered through the gate. Even though Champtown was a big guy, he wrestled his way through the gate and we stood there on the other side. We had just trespassed onto Paisley Park. My heart was pounding. I didn't say anything out loud because I didn't want to look soft in front of my homeboy, but on the inside I was panicking. I expected security to be on us at any minute.

But Champtown was as cool a guy as you could find. Nothing seemed to rile him. He calmly walked towards the building entrance and pulled on the darkly tinted glass doors. Locked. No surprise there. I cupped my hands around my eyes and peered through the glass. I could see the outer part of the atrium, which was overseen by a mural of Prince's doe-like eyes amidst a sea of clouds. That was where Prince had been interviewed by Oprah back in 1996. I couldn't believe it. I was actually at Paisley Park! Even if I was basically breaking and entering.

I got a few pictures of myself outside the Park and then we left, driving back to Minneapolis. We went to a bar and grill in an industrial part of the city and while I waited for my burger and beer to be delivered to the table, Champtown was texting with someone I was familiar with—Violent J.

By some convoluted twist of fate, I had managed to squash a rap beef between ICP and Champtown that went back years. I can't remember what started the beef, but it went back to the very beginning of ICP's career. On the song "Never Had it Made" on the ICP album *Carnival of Carnage* there's a diss aimed at Champtown's mother. While I'd been researching the Danny KAE story for Metro Times, I let it be known to both Champtown and the Clowns that I'd been in contact with the other party. Champtown wanted to interview ICP for a documentary about Detroit hip-hop but he didn't know how to reach out to the Clowns. I mentioned this to Violent J and he said to have Champtown give him a call. He did and a twenty year plus rap beef fizzled away.

So now Champtown and Violent J were friendly. As they texted, I asked Champtown to ask Violent J if I could get his email address, as I had some ideas I wanted to run by him. Violent J, who knew me as "the Danny KAE guy," agreed and when I got home to Dayton, I sent him an email with a series of Juggalo-related ideas. Ideas for T-shirts, ideas for songs to sample, and especially, ways to fight back against the FBI for the stupid "Juggalos are a gang" designation.

In 2011, Juggalos had been labelled a "loosely organized hybrid gang" in a national gang task force report. While ICP initially took the news in stride and even bemusement, they weren't laughing when they heard report after report of Juggalos getting the bone from law enforcement simply for wearing ICP gear or getting pulled over and searched for having an ICP bumper sticker on their car.

A few days after I sent Violent J the email, I got an excited response. First, he congratulated me on the Metro Times Danny KAE story, calling it "the shit," which I took as high praise. He also invited me to come to Farmington Hills, Michigan for a meeting with him, Shaggy, and the label heads.

I couldn't believe it. One of my favorite rappers in the whole wide world wanted a meeting with me. I pulled myself together and put together a list of ideas for the label. Products they should bring back. Products they should release. Just as many ideas as I could think of. I knew not all of these would make an impact but I figured it was better to have too many ideas than not enough.

I borrowed a suit jacket from my old boss Mark and drove up to Farmington Hills, which was about a half hour outside of Detroit. Swallowing my jitters, I went inside the unassuming looking office building on a frontage road and I was introduced to Joseph Bruce—aka Violent J—as well as his brother Rob/Jumpsteady, and the label CEO William Dail, better known as Billy Bill.

I took a deep breath, swallowed, and gave them my pitch at a big conference room table. I was well-prepared and tackled the meeting as if my life depended on it. At the end of my presentation of ideas,

Violent J seemed really impressed, telling me "Man, you gotta be one of the most professional ninjas we've ever spoken to." After the meeting, Violent J took me around Psychopathic Records, showing me the warehouse where they shipped merchandise all over the world. There were literally wall-to-wall shelves of T-shirts, jerseys, thongs, hats, you name it. No one did merchandise quite like ICP, except maybe KISS. It was quite a sight to behold.

I shook hands with everybody, thanked them, and headed towards the door. Before I left, though, I asked for—and got—a quick picture with Violent J, which in hindsight was not very professional, but hey, once a Juggalo, always a Juggalo.

Weeks went by and I didn't hear anything. I followed up with emails to Billy and Violent J, trying to make sure they didn't forget me while at the same time, trying not to be annoying. One day when I was at a Kia car dealership getting the engine of my 2008 Rio repaired for what seemed like the hundredth time, I got a call from Billy.

"Hey, J-Webb, when could you start?"

I silently bit my lip and did a Snoopy dance outside the dealership as I took the phone call I'd been working towards my whole life. Billy and I briefly discussed salary, agreed on a fair number, and I told him I could be relocated to Detroit in a month. That was that. I was an official employee of Psychopathic Records, my favorite rap label.

"I've made it!" I said to my friend Erin over the phone. Erin was a former co-worker of mine from my editor days and we kept up with each other's post-City Paper successes. Erin had graduated from the improv program at Second City in Chicago, and I was really proud of her. As I dazzled her with my own triumph, she said something prophetic: "Just be careful. You've seen the movies. You know the music industry is a crazy place."

XIII.

One of my favorite comedies is "This Is Spinal Tap." But for the five years I worked for Psychopathic Records, I couldn't bring myself to watch the film. The line between tragedy and comedy is extremely thin, and what once drove me to laughter now only made me cringe like I was listening to the sound of scratching sandpaper. The scene with Nigel and the small bread? That shit happens. So does getting lost under the stage, arguments with distributors over tasteless artwork, and dealing with hotel rooms not being ready. Next to politics, the music industry was the toughest gig I ever worked.

But it was an experience I wouldn't have dared miss.

I committed a faux pas right out of the gate on my first day at Psychopathic Records. I showed up in a suit. Jacket, tie, polished shoes, the works. And when I saw Shaggy he burst into laughter.

"Damn, J-Webb, what's up with the suit? You look like you have to go to court." Oh, shit. I got weird looks from the other people in the office and Rob straight up told me, "You know, J-Webb, you don't have to wear a suit." I never made that mistake again.

There's no training program or grace period when you work for Psychopathic Records. They pick you up, throw you into the deep end of the pool, and see if you sink or swim. I mostly dog paddled in the beginning. I quickly realized that my images of staying on the phone all day talking with news editors and program directors in the name of spreading the Dark Carnival gospel to the media outlets of America was an illusion. At Psychopathic, you were expected to wear a lot of different hats—sometimes literally if the Clowns needed you to be a zombie in their show; this happened to me a few times and it was both wonderful and surreal to perform with Violent J and Shaggy.

Though I'd been supposedly hired to do media work, I did anything and everything at Psychopathic. I found myself loading and unloading pallets and pallets of Faygo, the cheap, Detroit-made soft drink that ICP sprayed on their audience as their signature concert tradition.

As the holidays approached, I was downstairs in the warehouse, helping pull and pack merchandise orders from Juggalos all over the world. When there was a Detroit event, such as a concert or a Juggalo wrestling match, I would be tasked out to do everything from carve pumpkins, to stuff a scarecrow, to round up towels, makeup remover, and clothing for the Clown's performance that night. But mostly I was sent on missions to do something damn near impossible. Like the time I had to procure two authentic black hooded monk robes with one day's notice before ICP's sold out "Riddlebox" show at St. Andrew's Hall.

As CEO, Billy ran a tight ship at Psychopathic. He was the furthest thing from a micromanager as you could get, but he wasn't afraid to push you to your limits. An imposing stocky figure always dressed in a black T-shirt, black cap, and a scowl, Billy expected results. No costume shops within 100 miles had any monk robes, not that something like that would ever stop a Psychopathic Records employee. Stories about employees driving several states away to secure a prop for show were commonplace. You did what you had to do to make sure the show went on.

After exhausting Google and making an estimated 20 phone calls all over the state, I found a guy who carried real cloth monk robes. The problem is, he only had one black one and I needed two. He had a white robe, which I bought, figuring we could dye it.

Before I left, the smartassed robe guy, who ran a games business out of his house in Lansing, asked me, "Hey, you work for the Insane Clown Posse, right?"

"Yeah. Why?" I replied.

"Aren't they terrorists?"

"Huh? What do you mean?" What the fuck was this guy talking about?

"Well, I saw on the news they were a terrorist organization or something. I don't want to be supporting terrorism."

I couldn't believe what I was hearing. "No, you heard about that stupid gang label by the FBI. That's a total crock of crap. ICP is a music brand nothing more."

The guy laughed slightly. "Well, OK, but aren't their shows really violent?"

"Violent how?"

"Well, you know, like people beat each other up and stuff like that."

I shook my head. "That's called 'moshing.' ICP didn't invent that, believe me."

The guy still didn't look convinced. "Well, that's fine. I just gotta make sure I'm not contributing to something bad, y'know?"

I'm sure I was looking at the man with an incredulous look on my face. "Tomorrow night, there will be over a thousand people enjoying a music show. That's all. And you will have played a part in it by hooking us up with these robes."

"Hmmm. Well, OK. Good luck with the show."

I stormed off the guy's property seething. So that's what people thought of ICP? I knew Juggalos were probably the most reviled and hated fanbase in music history, owing to Juggalos' reputation for being loud, obnoxious, and committing the occasional act of vagrancy, but "terrorists?" I started to take what I was supposed to be doing as Director of Public Relations (said so right on my business card) seriously right then and there. Before that moment, working for

ICP felt like a fanboy getting a peek behind the scenes at his favorite band. But after that guy's "terrorist" comment, my job with ICP felt like a calling, some kind of holy quest.

But first I had to deal with the problem at hand: Dyeing a white robe black. I managed to find a sketchy looking carpet store that agreed to do it out in Hazel Park, not too far from where Selena used to live. The grungy looking guy who ran the place smelled like cigarettes and sweat and told me the robe would be ready the next morning. Fuck! That was the day of the show!

I arrived at the carpet store the next morning, promptly at 8 a.m. and discovered that robe, which was still soaking wet, was not black, but a dark gray charcoal color. Double fuck! Not only was the robe the wrong color, but there was no way it could've been line dried by the time we had to get all the stage props down to the venue. Or could it? I drove back to the office, lugged the garbage bag full of wet cloth to the warehouse and set up a few space heaters to try and dry it out. Hours went by and it was still wet, but I was able to get it dry enough to be damp. Whoever had to wear this wasn't going to be happy.

But that wasn't the end of my problems. I got a text from Billy simply saying "get down to the venue we need you." That sent my anxiety into super overdrive and I felt like I was working for Carty again. Not because Billy was being mean, but because I was shaking and couldn't stop. I was a mess of nerves, fear, and caffeine from stealing too many of Violent J's sugar free Red Bulls.

I drove to St. Andrew's Hall doing 90 the whole way there, and I wasn't usually the kind of driver who was a speeder. When I got there, I was greeted by my co-worker Kandi, who also happened to be Billy's girlfriend.

"Where you been? We've been looking for you," Kandi said in a deadpan voice that always sounded irritated. It was obvious she didn't like me, even though I tried to be nice to her. I ran up to Billy when I saw him hanging out by the soundboard.

Billy wasn't the type of guy for pleasantries. "Need you to go back to office and get Joe's mic stand. We brought the wrong one." Fuck. That meant I was going to have to pay for parking again. I ran out the door, back to the parking lot, which cost $20 to park, and headed back to the office. It took 40 minutes to drive back to Farmington Hills due to rush hour traffic. The mic stand in question was standing by the back garage door of the far end of the warehouse where we usually stored the pallets of Faygo. It was covered from top to bottom with green and purple electrical tape—the color scheme of the Riddle Box character that defined ICP's third album.

I felt my phone buzz with a text message. I pulled it out of my pocket and looked at it. It was Billy with another one of his trademarked to-the-point messages.

"hurry up"

Fuck! My anxiety was only raging more out of control. Plus, I could barely fit the mic stand into my car, eventually wedging it between the front passenger seat and the driver's side of the back seat.

I roared back to St. Andrew's Hall, stopping at a drive-through ATM to get more money out so I could pay for parking. Again. After parking my car and once again paying $20 to the attendant, I wrestled the mic stand out of the car. I walked past the line of Juggalos who were waiting to get into the venue, hearing constant refrains of "Whoop! Whoop!," the Juggalo battle cry. I went past security who thankfully didn't hassle me. I had never been in the backstage area of St. Andrew's so I felt like an idiot wandering around aimlessly carrying the awkward-sized mic stand.

"J-Webb!"

It was Cash, one of Billy's stagehands. Cash was also an amazing drummer and had actually been a tour musician for Dennis De Young. Cash ran up to me and took the mic stand off my hands.

"Go find Billy. He's looking for you." I felt my stomach knot up as I once again went meandering around the backstage looking for Billy. I found him over by the stage door and he looked pissed.

"Where you been?" he said in his soft voice that always sent a chill down my spine. Without meaning to, he always sounded like Jake "The Snake" Roberts.

"I went to the office to get the mic stand and I had to find Cash to give it to him and ..."

"OK, Jason, I get it," said Billy. "Here" he said, handing me a stack of bills. "Go downstairs to the merch stand and help sell merch." I took the money, stuffed it into the pocket of my Levi's and headed towards the stairs to The Shelter, the venue in the basement of St. Andrew's. When I saw the walls and tables of merchandise, I gulped. I watched my co-workers Will and Tom behind the table, deftly and expertly selling T-shirts, hats, jewelry, and CDs to dozens of excited Juggalos, all bunched up together in front of the stand. Here was the problem: I couldn't do math in my head. Never been able to. If you bought a T-shirt for $30, a hat for $20, and a Psychopathic Records logo charm for $14 from me, there was no way I'd be able to calculate all that without writing it down.

I swallowed my anxiety as best I could, and climbed under the table to emerge on the other side of the stand. It was surreal—for years I'd just been another Juggalo buying merch, now I was selling it.

"What up, my ninja?" I hollered out to the dreadlocked Juggalo couple in front of me.

"Riddle Box Show shirt. 3XL. A knit hat. A girl's shirt."

"OK, what size?"

"Large. No, better make it XL."

OK, 3XL Riddle Box shirt. I started to dig around the box of shirts sitting on the ground. Problem was, the shirts were all jumbled up together. I pawed through the black tees seeing a lot of XLs and 2XLs, but no 3XLs. Panicked, I continued to look for the shirt but came up empty.

"Do we have any 3XL Riddle Box shirts?!" I asked both Tom and Will.

"Yeah, they're in there." Fuck. I dove into the box of shirts again and I finally found a 3XL. OK, great. Got it. Ummmm…shit. I couldn't remember what else that couple wanted.

"Ummmmm…you wanted a ball cap, right?"

"No, dog, a knit hat!"

A Riddle Box knit hat. Right. At least I knew where that was. And I remembered they wanted a girly shirt too. An XL. I spun around and grabbed the two pieces of merch from off the back table. OK. It was math time. $30 for the T-shirt, $20 for the knit hat … shit, how much was the girly shirt? Check the wall. $24. OK, so that's $50 plus $24. $74! Thank God it was a simple equation.

"That'll be $74, homies." The dude handed me a $100 bill. I had to count on my fingers, but I was able to figure out his change without a calculator.

"Here you go, ninjas!" I handed the merch and change to the couple, grateful that the transaction went off without a snag. I stepped up to the next Juggalo and asked what they wanted. I was able to maintain a steady pace, even though Will and Tom were selling stuff so quickly they were practically a blur. A few times I had to break out my iPhone and use the calculator, but thankfully I got through the frenzy of merch selling.

I leaned against the merch table and took an exhausted breath. I felt my phone buzz in my pocket from a text message.

"come here."

Shit. Every time Billy texted me I felt like I was getting called down to the principal's office. I ran upstairs and found Billy by the soundboard.

"Hey, did you dry that robe? Rob says it's still wet."

"Well, it's damp, yeah. I had it set up with some space heaters, but…"

Billy looked at me with his beady eyes, and a faint smile.

"Jason … it's not damp. It's wet."

I shrugged and threw my hands up in a "what do you want me to do?" way.

"I…I had the space heater on it for hours, man."

"OK, we'll deal with it," said Billy, turning away from me. The conversation was done. Could … I leave? His attention focused on the soundboard, I slowly crept away in case Billy had something else he wanted to talk to me about. Carty had been the same way. If you left prematurely, he would give you a verbal thrashing. I silently cursed thinking about Carty and the fact that I was still shellshocked from working for him years after I'd left his employ.

But this time, I appeared to be free to go. I wandered around the sold-out St. Andrew's capacity crowd, admiring the Juggalos who showed up in full regalia. I went to the bar and got myself a beer and stood towards the back of the venue waiting for the show to start.

About a half hour later, the lights dimmed and the chaos and ludicrousness of an Insane Clown Posse show overtook the room. Faygo. Chicken feathers. Streamers. More Faygo. Lots and lots more Faygo. The Clowns went through about 500 two-liters of diet Faygo cola and root beer each show. They almost always used diet Faygo because the sugar from the regular brand ate away at the foam rubber of their stage sets.

As I soaked up the spectacle of the show, I looked around at the crowd and realized something: I'd made a dream come true. I had always wanted to work for my favorite rap group and now I was. I smiled as I considered this and enjoyed the rest of the night. I'd survived working my first big ICP show.

At work the next day, I attacked my public relations duties with the fervor and devotion of a religious acolyte. And it paid off. Over the course of my five-year tenure with the Clowns, I got ICP feature-length interviews with The New York Times, VICE, and Rolling Stone. I got them on The Howard Stern Show. I even got Violent J a chance to write a guest editorial about the FBI gang label bullshit for Time magazine. I was a damn good publicist, ensuring that wherever they went on tour, the town knew the Dark Carnival was coming.

I got better at working at concerts, even though I never could get the hang of selling merch. I also was put in charge of project management for all ICP releases, from CDs to DVDs to even the long-awaited ICP boxed set, which collected ICP's first six albums for the first time ever.

I helped out at the annual Gathering of the Juggalos music festival, ensuring we got plenty of positive news coverage, and when Juggalos marched on Washington, D.C. to protest the FBI gang label in September of 2017, I was one of the main architects behind the event. I even got my name in the Wikipedia article on "Juggalo March."

And through it all, Prince continued to exert his purple influence upon my life.

XIV.

_T_owards the end of 2014, I got one of the most important gifts of my life. My co-worker Will, who sewed most of ICP's clown suits, happened upon a beautiful crushed velvet Purple Rain outfit at a costume shop that was going out of business. He bought the suit for me because he knew I'd love it; that was Will for you.

When he presented me with the outfit, I got teary eyed. No one had ever gifted me something so amazing. I was still pretty skinny back then and the suit was a little bit baggy on me, but no matter. I loved the suit and couldn't wait to wear it for Halloween. But I luckily got my chance to wear it sooner thanks to the Gathering of the Juggalos.

Rob decided that year we would have a Juggalo Wedding. This non-binding ceremony provided a chance for a great spectacle, including a food fight with the cake. Rob decided we also needed an additional touch: Prince.

The plan was me and a woman would do a duet of the Prince song "U Got the Look" on the stage as part of the pre-wedding flavor. While everyone took their places at the altar, we would be bumping and grinding our way through the song. I didn't need a rehearsal; I'd been singing that song since 1987. But what about my duet partner? I wouldn't be seeing her until the day of the performance. I knew she was a member of the rap group entourage Wolfpac and Rob showed me her picture—she was gorgeous with braided hair and an athletic body—but could she sing? Hell, could I sing? Doing Prince karaoke in a bar on a Friday night was one thing, but singing in front of hundreds of Juggalos was something else entirely.

Planning and executing the Gathering of the Juggalos was always done by the seat-of-your-pants. You had to be ready for anything and everything to happen, because it usually would. I had gone from attending the first two Gatherings as just another Juggalo to working behind the scenes to help make them happen. It was always the hardest work you did all year, but man oh man, it was so worth it when you saw all the happy Juggalos having the time of their lives.

When the day finally came, I was ready. I had a karaoke version of "U Got the Look" burned onto a CD to hand to the DJ. I was dressed head to toe in my Purple Rain outfit—velvet pull-on pants with big oversized buttons, a silky ivory colored ruffled poet shirt, just like the one Prince wore in "Purple Rain," and a beautiful jacket. I completed the ensemble with a pair of purple suede sneakers, also courtesy of Will, a black curly wig, and a pair of round Lennon-style purple lensed sunglasses.

I met my duet partner, a great woman named Scarlet, before the wedding was scheduled to kick off. We shook hands, exchanged smiles, and engaged in pleasant chitchat. She assured me she knew the Sheena Easton part and had been practicing for weeks.

"I wasn't really a Prince fan before I learned this song, but I am now," she said.

I smiled. "I've been looking forward to this all year."

We pulled off the song perfectly and were the hit of the faux wedding.

The next time I wore the Purple Rain suit was for an even more amazing reason: Prince was coming back to Detroit for the first time in 11 years! Even though tickets were $200, I bought one the moment they went on sale. I decided then and there that I had to wear my suit to the concert, even though I'd heard stories of Prince having people thrown out of the venue if he encountered a looka-like. Champtown told me an amazing story about this cat named Rodney L. who as early as the *Dirty Mind* days used to copy Prince's manner of dress. According to Champtown, Rodney L. showed up at Prince's Detroit show of the *Dirty Mind* tour, dressed in full Prince regalia and Prince saw him in the front row and asked security to get rid of him because he was causing too much of a distraction. Prince also personally confronted Rodney L. and demanded to know why he was mimicking his manner of dress. But that didn't stop Rodney L. He was basically a Prince-miming performance artist, copying most of Prince's looks over the years. I met Rodney L. a few years back when Champtown got me backstage to Ice-T's "The Art of Rap" tour—he was sporting a typhoon-style hairdo like Prince wore in the *Diamonds and Pearls* days.

So I didn't want Prince to give me the Rodney L. treatment. I didn't think there was much of a chance though, because I was back pretty far from the stage. But I was still nervous to wear the suit just in case Prince saw it.

No matter, though. The day of the concert came and I hitched a ride with Violent J and his wife Michelle, who was better known in the Juggalo world as Sugar Slam. When Violent J saw me dressed in a Prince costume he laughed uproariously.

"J-Webb, you really have a screw loose!" he exclaimed. I just smiled. I couldn't argue with the guy. Before we went to the venue, I had dinner with Violent J and Michelle. It was rare to get a chance to just sit with one of my favorite rappers and just shoot the shit. We talked about Prince, Michael Jackson, Danny KAE; it felt like two friends catching up after years of being apart. Both Violent J and Shaggy were always nice to me. A few professional disagreements over the years, but I have nothing but love for both of those guys.

When we got to the Fox Theater in Downtown Detroit, I was mobbed by Prince fans who wanted their picture with me. It was a fun feeling. I happily posed for pictures with dozens of smiling faces and everyone complimented me on my outfit.

Little did I know that Prince's show in Detroit at the Fox Theater on April 9, 2015 would be the last time the man would perform in the Motor City. I'm just so glad I got to witness it. It wasn't my favorite live performance of Prince, but the show still kicked plenty of ass. Now dressed in hippy threads and sporting a perfectly round Afro, Prince not only performed all the hits, but many surprises including effective covers of Stargard's "Which Way Is Up?" and Janet Jackson's "What Have You Done For Me Lately?" For me, the crowing moment of the night was when Prince sat at the piano and performed "The Love We Make," one of my favorite songs of all time; the next day, Violent J asked me "Damn, J-Webb, what was that piano song Prince played towards the end?!" It was a truly spine-tingling performance.

After the show, though, I broke Violent J's heart. We were all in his big black Suburban van going back to Farmington Hills, when an awe-filled Violent J started imagining out loud what Prince was doing at that moment.

"Man, you just know Prince is getting his dick sucked right now."

I knew this wasn't happening. And for some reason, I stupidly felt compelled to say something.

"Well, actually, Prince is celibate these days so I'm pretty sure that's not true."

Violent J was incredulous upon hearing this news.

"What the fuck do you mean he's celibate? There's no way."

"Yeah, man, it's crazy but since he converted to the Jehovah's Witnesses, he says he's celibate."

Violent J shook his head and exhaled with disappointment. "Fuck, J-Webb, why'd you have to tell me that? That totally killed my buzz." I felt awful. Violent J was a great guy, but he could also be really sensitive. I kept my mouth shut for the rest of the ride back to his house, feeling like an ass.

Occasional faux pas aside, I was doing really well at Psychopathic Records. Everyone seemed to respect me, even Kandi seemed to warm up to me. I convinced the label to start reissuing ICP's old albums on remastered vinyl, which paid off handsomely. I also got to oversee special anniversary boxed sets of both *The Riddle Box* and *The Great Milenko*, both of which were big feathers in my professional cap.

Here's a funny story from the ICP years. I was in Los Angeles with the Clowns doing press for their TV show on Fuse, "Insane Clown Posse Theater," which lasted two seasons; in fact, the show was never cancelled because it did very well in the ratings, but Fuse changed management and the new brass simply never got back to Psychopathic about a third season. Anyway, we're out there in L.A. and it's getting to be dinnertime and Violent J wanted to go back to his hotel room. He asked me to get him a salad and an order of chicken wings and deliver it to his room. Me, Shaggy, and ICP's assistant Chop all went out to eat at a diner, and I ordered Violent J's food to go. I got back to the hotel with the food and knocked on his door. I heard a mumbled voice but couldn't make out what was being said. I knocked again, a little louder. More mumbling from the other side of the door. I waited about two minutes and then knocked again. What the fuck was going on? Suddenly the door opened up a crack and Violent J's thundering voice boomed down the hallway.

"Leave it outside the DOOR! I'M NAKED!"

I dutifully placed the salad and wings on the floor in front of the door and scattered away, not wanting to have to face a nude insane clown, but not before seeing someone down the hall open their hotel room door and look out to see what the commotion was. No one said working in showbusiness was all glitz and glamour.

Despite experiencing fun moments like a nude Violent J while working for Psychopathic Records, all was not well. I was burned out, once again addicted to Xanax, and riddled with depression and anxiety. But I suddenly found myself dealing with something even crazier than anything related to Insane Clown Posse: Fatherhood.

XV.

I never wanted to be a dad. Ever.

My own experiences with paternal forces and seeing what other people went through with their kids had turned me into something of a Peter Pan. Fatherhood was for people who wanted to pass something on to the next generation, carry on their family name, or some other sentimental bullshit. The only things I wanted to pass on were my concert T-shirt collection to my nephew and my DVD collection to my sister if she wanted it. I had no desire whatsoever to procreate. I was an overgrown child myself, shaped by family trauma and dysfunction. What the hell would I do with a kid?

The first 20 years of my life had been a royal clusterfuck, so I spent the next 20 years trying to make up for my childhood and lost adolescence. This expressed itself in a brash, haughty attitude and a strong contempt for authority that was often overwhelming for both myself and others.

But all that posturing came to an end one October night in 2014. I was at some chain bistro that me and this girl Jane went to on the regular. I'd met Jane on OKCupid or some similar dating app the previous fall and we had a nice connection. There were lots of day trips to antique stores, martini bars, coffee shops, and the same mom-n-pop diner for breakfast every Saturday morning.

Meantime, I was nursing an ever-growing Xanax dependency. The music industry was a tough gig and I was suffering from near terminal burnout. My doctor once again prescribed me Xanax, and even though I was nervous to take them again after going through a mild addiction during the Carty years, I couldn't deny they helped keep my anxiety at bay. Jane helped with that, too. She was beautiful with dark brown hair, a fine body—she played roller derby—and was one of the funniest women I'd ever dated, with the driest wit imaginable.

But as we sat there across from each other, she wasn't smiling. She was uncharacteristically quiet and something was up. I assumed she'd had a shitty day at the grocery store she managed, and that was it. But it was something decidedly different.

"So I took a test. It's positive," she said in a deadpan voice.

I'm not sure if it was pure shock or stupidity but her statement didn't register with me.

"What kind of test?" I asked.

Jane just looked at me for a beat. "A pregnancy test."

Upon hearing those words, I took a long drink on my water that was resting on the table. And at that moment our server decided to pay us a visit.

"Well, hi!" she exclaimed, all big smile and blonde hair. "What are you two troublemakers up to this evening?"

Her jovial, over-the-top nature rubbed me the wrong way since I was still recoiling from the truth bomb Jane had dropped.

"Yeah, let me get a vodka martini. Extra olives."

"OK, sounds good. And for you?"

Jane didn't break her gaze at me. "I'll just have a Coke" she said icily.

"OK! I'll be right back." The server skipped away leaving us alone. I just stared at the table, my heart practically in my throat. Jane said nothing. Finally, I croaked out a sentence. It turned out to be the wrong one.

"Did you take a second one just to be sure?" Jane looked at me with daggers in her eyes. "Yes. I did the whole box. They all came up positive."

"So what do you want to do?" I asked.

Jane looked down. "Well, I'm not going to get an abortion, if that's what you're asking."

I panicked on the inside, because, well, that's *exactly* what I was asking.

"I wouldn't dream of asking you to do that," I lied. "I'm just asking, I mean, what about us? We're not exactly an official couple. What does this mean for you and I?"

Jane paused.

"Well, I guess that's up to you."

I searched my thoughts and feelings. The thought of being a father scared the shit out of me. I'd become one of them. A suburban dad with a bloated body, mowing the grass on weekends, and taking the kid to the zoo. I saw those type of men every day; hell, my dad was one of those men. And that was exactly why I had vowed to never join their ranks. I didn't want to be henpecked, spineless, or just have my life become a to-do-list of parental stuff ranging from dentist appointments to hosting kid birthday parties.

But the last thing I could do was lay all this on Jane right about now. She needed me to be strong and for me to act like I had my shit together. I may have been renting a room and pissing into a Perrier bottle next to my bed and been perfectly happy with that arrangement but there was a good chance that was going to change whether I liked it or not.

"I'm in," I said, trying to convince myself I really was. "We'll figure it out."

At that moment, our perky server returned to the table with our drinks. I instantly took a big swallow of my martini. Vodka and vermouth had never tasted so good.

"Are we ready to order some food?" asked the server in her friendly manner.

"Ummm…You wanna just share an order of potstickers?" I asked Jane, realizing that neither of us had even bothered to look at the menu because we were both too busy staring at the table.

"Sure," said Jane, with nary an ounce of enthusiasm.

"OK. We'll take the Asian potstickers, please," I said to the ever-smiling server. "And another martini, please."

"You got it! I'll be right back with that."

As soon as the server had left, I grabbed the stem of my martini glass and drained it dry. The bitterness of the alcohol made my body shudder. And suddenly I had a thought about Prince.

On his debut album *For You*, there was a song called "Baby," in which Prince sings to a girl he's accidentally gotten pregnant. There at the table, I started playing the song in my head, finding it darkly humorous that I was in this situation. I hadn't exactly been a stickler for birth control when I'd been with Jane, so what was I expecting would happen?

"So are we going to be a family?" asked Jane suddenly, snapping me out of my Prince reverie.

"Yeah, we are," I said, not knowing if I was telling the truth or not.

When the server brought the potstickers, I could barely touch them, despite not having eaten all day. We pecked away at the thoroughly mediocre appetizer and mostly just sat in silence. I could hear my heartbeat ringing in my ears. Finally, we just paid the bill and left the restaurant. I walked Jane back to her car, awkwardly putting my arm around her.

"It's gonna be OK," I reassured her. "We'll get through this."

"What do you mean?" said Jane, shaking my arm off and taking her keys out of her purse.

"Well, I mean, we'll get through it, you know? We'll figure something out."

This response was apparently not what Jane wanted to hear.

"Jason, this isn't something we just 'figure out.' I know you didn't plan on being a dad, but it appears that life has other plans in store for us. So what exactly do you think you're going to 'figure out?'"

"Ummm, well, I mean…" I stuttered trying to string some semblance of a sentence together. I just dropped it. I sounded like an idiot and I knew it. I gave Jane a stiff hug and watched her start up her car and drive away.

Needless to say, I had a hard time sleeping that night. I laid in bed processing a thousand what-ifs. Here I was pushing 40 and I had gotten a woman pregnant. I still couldn't process the "going to be a dad" part.

Around 3:30 in the morning, I got up, logged into my computer and went to my iTunes. I listened to "Baby" by Prince a few times on repeat.

But the next morning, I made a total ass of myself. It was around 7 a.m. and I'd slept for about an hour all night long. I grabbed my phone and texted Jane.

> Hey jane. So ive slept on it and I have to tell you that I think we're in a serious bind here. The fact is I don't want to be a father. I have no idea how to be a good dad. I'm just not father material. Some men are. Im not. If we go through with this, we're going to regret it. Both of us. I dont want either of us to throw our lives away over a mistake. Can we get together tonight and talk about this some more?

A minute went by. Then another minute. Right when I was starting to get itchy and wonder how long it was going to be for Jane to respond, she did. And she officially schooled my ass.

> Jason I am not getting an abortion. That's final. If you don't want to have any part of this baby, that's entirely up to you. I'm not forcing you into anything. I'm having this baby because I feel that it's the right thing for me

to do. I may never have this opportunity ever again. I can go to the court and have them void your rights as the father. If I do that, you will never see me or the baby again. But if that's what you want, I'll totally do that. I'm not twisting your arm. It's up to you. I don't want to get together tonight.

Well, fuck. I had just made a royal ass of myself and was acting like a total shithead. What was I supposed to do? I was going to be a fucking father and if I signed away my parental rights, I knew exactly where I'd end up–stalking Jane and the kid for the rest of my life. I shuddered at the thought of that; the whole idea just repulsed me. I was already embarrassed enough that I was acting so stupid. Time to grow up, Webber, I said to myself. You're gonna be a dad, so you better make the most of it.

Later that day after I got home from work, I laid on my bed and asked myself: How would Prince handle this situation?

Prince had never gotten the chance to be a dad. When his son died a few days after birth, Prince apparently went into a tailspin that he never really recovered from. According to Mayte's book *The Most Beautiful*, published the year after Prince died, the death of their baby drove a serious wedge in between the couple. Mayte had a miscarriage in the year following the baby's death, which only divided them further. It seems like something as traumatic as the death of one's child would either bring the couple together and bind them to one another even more closely, or it would split the couple apart. The latter is what Mayte said happened to her and Prince.

I thought about how much Prince wanted to be a father. *Emancipation* is a total valentine to Mayte and their then impending parenthood. And Prince came from an abusive, dysfunctional family, yet he still wanted kids. I tried to wrap my arms around that. Why would Prince want to be a father if his own paternal role models hadn't been all that great? Maybe it was because he thought if he had children of his own and did a better job than his father and step-father did, maybe it could help heal his inner child. Or something like that. I didn't know shit about why men wanted to be fathers. Maybe it was because I was adopted and had pretty complicated feelings about it, but I just couldn't fathom the idea of why people wanted kids. Sure, our bodies were made to produce offspring, so having a child was about as natural as blinking your eyes or breathing. But that didn't make it any easier for me to deal with.

Over the course of the next nine months, though, I got better. Jane and I moved into her cramped one-bedroom bungalow in Troy. As I got used to living with a woman again, I ever-so-slowly began to come around to the fact that I was going to be a father. As we entered the third trimester and Jane got as big as a house, I counted down the days until I would not only become a dad, but basically a grownup as well.

I could no longer live a life of living simply and spending all my money on music, pop culture memorabilia, and day trips to Ann Arbor. On one hand, I dreaded giving all that up, but on the other one, it was undeniably exciting to know that my future was going to change in a big way.

And on July 2, 2015, it did. Our daughter Kathleen was born at 8:25 p.m., following a labor that lasted a full two days. Watching her being born was pretty incredible. She had my eyes and mouth, and (thankfully) Jane's cute little nose. After I cut the cord and they had put Kathleen in the incubator to weigh and measure her, I went up to the little plastic crib and said a few words to my daughter, which went something like this:

"Hi. Well, kid, here's the deal. I don't know how to be a dad. Most of the dads I know suck. But then again, you don't know how to be a kid, do you? So how about this: I'll help you be a kid, if you help me be a dad. And we'll try and get through it together and figure something out. OK?"

It may have been my imagination, but I could've sworn that my daughter, just minutes old, looked at me and smiled.

I imagine that next to the moment of death and the moment of birth, the instant you become a parent has got to be the most surreal moment of your life. One minute you're just living for yourself, the next you are literally responsible for the health, survival, and upbringing of another human being. Your mind gets blown away daily by every new stage in your child's development, from the first dirty diaper to the first laugh to the first word; unsurprisingly, Kathleen's first word was "shit," which was bound to happen considering she was being raised by two world class cussers.

When Kathleen was born, I wasn't exactly in the best frame of mind. I'd stepped up and put my big boy pants on and was there for Jane and Kathleen, but my Xanax addiction was getting worse. During Jane's pregnancy, I'd gone from breaking off pieces of the bar a few times a day to just swallowing the bar whole. I was also starting to drink a lot, putting Irish cream or Rumchata into my morning coffee.

I'd do my job in a benzo haze and then go home and watch Kathleen while Jane rested. Neither of us got much sleep in those days, as anyone who's ever had a baby can attest to. But my Xanax dependency and drinking were making things worse.

It all came to a major head in the summer of 2016. Kathleen had just turned a year old. Prince and David Bowie had both passed away a few months earlier. My stress level at Psychopathic Records was going through the roof because we were working on putting on our annual Gathering of the Juggalos music festival. I was depressed, angry, and was starting to have little hope for the future. What kind of father was I? I was nothing but a pill popping drunk who was getting fatter every day. My moods were all over the place. Jane was starting to barely speak to me.

One night while Jane was at work and after I'd put Kathleen to bed, I was swigging from my bottle of Jack Daniels as per usual, when I decided to play a little game of roulette. I took two pieces from a Xanax bar and swallowed them down with a big gulp of whiskey. At the time, I didn't actively think to myself "I want to die" but if I did…it wouldn't have been a bad thing.

The next thing I remember is waking up on the bed with Jane shaking me awake. Apparently, I'd been out for a while and the only reason Jane didn't call an ambulance to take me away was that she could see I was still breathing. The next morning, though, my ass was in for it.

"What the fuck do you think you're trying to do?" Jane demanded. "You better give me one reason why I shouldn't call the hospital and have you committed." I didn't say anything, I just stared at the carpet.

"You need to go and talk to somebody and I mean it," Jane spat at me. "If you don't go get help, I'm not promising you that me and Kathleen are still going to be here. If you're going to kill yourself, you're doing it on your own. We're not going to be an accessory to it."

I knew she was right. I did need help. And this time I needed answers. Real answers. I was tired of every time I went to a shrink they'd want to talk about my childhood, or talk about my job. Whatever was wrong with me was more than just depression. There was something more, I just knew it. And I had to find out what it was.

The next day, I looked up a psychiatrist in my insurance network and made an appointment. I can't remember what the guy's name was but he was really friendly and didn't pussyfoot around. I told him about the half-assed suicide attempt and he asked me a few questions about my moods. Did I have trouble sleeping? Were there times I couldn't remember things? I got the feeling we were on the right track, because the doctor was asking all the right things.

Finally after about 45 minutes, the doctor told me he had a diagnosis: Borderline Personality Disorder, the same thing Glenn Close had in "Fatal Attraction." It was all there. The suicidal idealization. The on-a-dime mood swings. I finally had a name for the demon that had plagued me all those years. I knew all along it was more than just clinical depression. I angrily thought back to all the counselors and shrinks I'd been to over the years—how come none of them had diagnosed me with BPD?

I quickly got on a new pill called Abilify, which acted as a mood stabilizer. The new med combined with regular therapy helped enormously and I started to slowly feel better. I stopped drinking as much and I decided to cut out the Xanax altogether. After a few months of weaning myself down to only one piece of the bar per day, I was eventually off it altogether. Instead, I discovered the miracle of CBD oil and used that twice a day. It worked. I haven't touched that bastard Xanax since.

Life was starting to turn around. I was starting to get a better handle on being a father. My relationship with Jane had strengthened. I was off the pills and booze. I finally had a great shrink who specialized in the treatment of personality disorders. And then the gravy train was abruptly stopped by the reintroduction of a shadowy figure from my past.

My birth mother.

XVI.

$\mathcal{W}$hen you're adopted, your life is an unfinished painting. Your adoptive parents fill in splashes of color and drawn in some shapes and try to give the image form, but the picture is far from complete. There's always the burning unanswered question of "Who am I?" in the back of your head, no matter how awesome your adoptive parents can be.

I'd spent my entire life wondering about my birth mother. I had a few clues to go on, but nothing concrete. In the mid- '90s, I'd contacted Ventura County social services about trying to get a copy of my original birth certificate, but after a dozen or so phone calls, I was told that all records pertaining to my birth were sealed barring a judge's order and the chance of a judge overturning the secrecy of a government-body sanctioned closed adoption from the '70s was practically nil.

But in the summer of 2018, thanks to Facebook, I got a lead. There was a woman named Diana who was an adoptee "search angel," meaning she specialized in reuniting adoptees with their birth information. She didn't have access to original birth certificates but she DID have birth records going back to the early 20th century. If you knew your birthdate and where you were born, she could cross-check the live births on that day, giving you a good idea who your parents probably were.

I emailed Diana and within only three hours, she had a hit. There was a birth on November 18, 1975 to a woman with the last name of Klaus and a man with the last name Estrada. That had to be them. The only clues I had to my real identity was that my birth father was Latinx and my mom was German. Surnames didn't get more respectfully ethnic sounding as Klaus and Estrada. That had to be them. It just had to be.

Diana did some more digging and after about a day, she'd narrowed it down that my birth mother was named Susan Klaus and my father was Jesus Estrada. I couldn't believe it. After years of wondering, I had names.

I got on Facebook and Google and set about doing some amateur internet sleuthing. Susan Klaus didn't have a Facebook or any real web presence to speak of. And there were quite a few Jesus Estradas in California. But something caught my eye as I browsed through the Facebook profiles: A nose.

There was a picture of an elderly Mexican man, probably in his late 60s, with black hair and eyes. He had a large honker of a nose with massive nostrils. It was the same exact nose that had gotten me teased both at school and at home. That was my nose. There was no question about it. This man was my father.

Jesus Estrada's profile was written entirely in Spanish and even though I had taken a few years of Spanish in both high school and college, I was anything but fluent. I decided against pursuing tracking him down any further, at least for now. I wanted to find my birth mother.

Susan Klaus was a bit more difficult to find. There were no pictures. No social media accounts. But there was an address and phone number in Ventura, California—my birthplace. I began to shake. Should I just call her? What was the proper protocol for a situation like this? Nothing can really prepare you for suddenly discovering who your birth parents are.

I decided to write her a letter and enclose a picture of myself; an approach I saw in the movie "Stuart Saves His Family" when Laura San Giacomo tracked down her birth father. I wrote a short and succinct letter to Susan Klaus and printed out a picture of me dressed up for my first day of work at Psychopathic, looking all nice in a suit. Figured that would make a good impression. In the letter, I introduced myself to my birth mother and invited her to call me or write me back.

Two weeks later, I was still waiting for a response. It was driving me crazy. She'd obviously gotten the letter—why wasn't I hearing anything back? Another week went by. Finally, I decided to just call her. I was tired of waiting. Maybe she was totally blown away and didn't know how to contact me or what to say to me. Hell, I didn't have a clue as to what I was going to say to her. I just wanted to hear her voice.

Fingers trembling, I dialed her number– calling a residential land line in the year 2018 was quite a novelty. The phone rang once. It rang twice. And then…

"Hello?" A woman's voice answered. This was it.

"Hi, Ms. Klaus? This is Jason Webber calling. I sent you a letter a few weeks back. I was just wondering if you'd received it."

There was a slight pause.

"Yes. And I am not interested in you at all."

Click went the phone as the line went dead.

My birth mom's words to me seemed to just hang there in the air. Yes. And. I. Am. Not. Interested. In. You. At. All. I'd waited 43 years to speak to my birth mother. I finally had. And it was all for nothing.

I sat there, not knowing what to think. I couldn't cry, I was too shocked and too numb. Besides, I wasn't going to let that woman wring a single tear from my eye. I meant nothing to her, so henceforward she would mean nothing to me.

I thought about my life for a second and then I realized I needed Prince. I wanted to lose myself in the sexy purple funk that had saved me so many times before. This flap with my birth mother was just another obstacle that I had to overcome. And the key to surmount-ing this staleness was a good Prince song. I got out my iPhone and pulled up Spotify and typed in a search for "The Love We Make," a beautiful, haunting piano ballad from *Emancipation* that Prince had performed the last time I saw him in concert. As I listened to the soothing lyrics about how the only love that exists in the world is "The Love We Make," it struck me that I needed to do something I'd been wanting to do for a while: I needed to make a pilgrimage to Paisley Park. I needed to visit the source of the purple flavor that had sustained me for all these years. And I needed to visit it soon.

XVII.

$\mathcal{I}$t was now the fall of 2018. Not only had my birth mother told me to fuck off, I was also told something similar by Psychopathic Records. They laid me and our web guy Dean off with little fanfare and I suddenly found myself moving back to Toledo. I wasn't thrilled about it, but I'd found a job there writing telephone marketing copy. I was making almost $20,000 less than I had been at Psychopathic Records, but it was the only job I could find.

I was broke, stressed, angry, and felt defeated. I could barely support a family on my salary, and I felt like a total loser for it. When I got my tax refund in early February, I decided on a total whim that I was going to go to Paisley Park. I needed some karma to perk me up and I knew that seeing Prince's home would do the trick. I was tired of waiting for "the right time." There would never be a "right time;" the only "right time" was the present.

I booked my plane ticket and reserved a hotel room without even telling Jane first. I also bought a ticket for the VIP tour of Paisley Park. That night when I told Jane, I halfway expected her to be mad, but instead she was understanding.

"You need to do this. You've been wanting to go there even before Prince died," Jane said. I loved Jane. She understood me like no one else ever could.

That night I went back and listened to some of the last albums that Prince recorded before he died: *PlectrumElectrum* and

ArtOfficialAge. At the time of their release, I was so busy working for the label that I barely had time to acknowledge these albums. The only music I was focusing on at that time was Insane Clown Posse and trying to convince the clowns that streaming and vinyl reissues of their old albums were the way of the future.

PlectrumElectrum was credited to 3rdeyegirl, Prince's new backing band, featuring a lean, mean rhythm section comprised of drummer Hannah Welton, guitarist Donna Grantis, and bassist Ida Kristine Nielsen. The album is largely an improvised funk and rock work, featuring a lot of loose guitar solos and jamming between Prince and the three musicians. Stripped down to the barest music essentials, Prince seems to be just plain having fun with this record. The songs are loose, raw, and carry an improvised feel, which is a far cry from the airtight, every-note-is-directed sounds of both The Revolution and The New Power Generation.

The album got mostly positive reviews although Rolling Stone only gave it two stars. I understood why some critics didn't take to the album—it's a pretty experimental piece of work, with no real hooks to hum. But it's an astonishing piece of work to listen to.

ArtOfficialAge was released on the same day as *PlectrumElectrum* and is definitely the more accessible of the two albums. It was more classic sounding Prince—lots of Linn drum machines and the classic "Minneapolis sound" that he had pioneered. I'll always remember this album as what was playing in Violent J's big Suburban truck when me, him, and Michelle all went to see Prince the last time he ever played in Detroit. Violent J really liked the song "Clouds," which is a smooth R&B mid-tempo jam in kind of the same vein as "Cream." My personal favorite on *ArtOfficialAge* is the silky-smooth lovemaking anthem "Breakfast Can Wait." Released as a single, the album art features Dave Chappelle dressed up as Prince holding a plate of pancakes. I literally laughed out loud the first time I saw it. Who said Prince doesn't have a sense of humor? Well, maybe "Weird Al"

Yankovic, since Prince never let him parody any of his songs, but that's another story.

I got up the next morning around 4 a.m. and got dressed in the dark so I wouldn't wake Jane. I grabbed my suitcase and popped into Kat's room and stared at her sleeping form in her day bed. "Bye, Kat," I whispered. "I love you."

After a groggy drive to the Detroit airport, I caught a Spirit Airlines flight to Minneapolis. For it being a February, the plane was surprisingly full, which I wasn't expecting considering it was so fucking cold. Dressed in my increasingly small-on-me overcoat and my Kangol driver cap, I got my rental car and prepared to drive into downtown Minneapolis. The city really reminded me of Toledo—cold, cozy, and predominantly blue collar. I drove to Electric Fetus, the indie record store Prince regularly shopped at. They had a whole section devoted to Prince—books, pins, shirts, coffee mugs. I bought a book called "Words of Prince" that I had never heard of, and bought used copies of the two albums that George Clinton had released on Paisley Park Records way back in the day, *The Cinderella Theory* and *Hey Man... Smell My Finger*, which to this day reigns as one of the best album titles of all time. I imagined Prince flipping through the vinyl and wondered if he ever went through his own section of albums. Their Prince section was, unsurprisingly, jammed with almost every Prince release that was in print, and even a few collector's items. They had a used CD copy of *The Black Album* for $30, which was a great price. It was downright surreal looking at Prince's music right in Minneapolis and it made me pause for a moment to reflect on how long I had wanted to be here. As a teenager, I used to have daydreams about hanging out in Minneapolis with fellow Prince fans and wondered if I'd ever have to chance to do that. And here I was.

While I was flipping through the reams of vinyl at Electric Fetus, I felt my cell phone buzz. It was Mom.

"Hi, Mom, how are you?"

"Well, HI!" she said in her trademark cheery voice. "What are you doing?"

"Ummm, I'm actually in Minneapolis right now. I'm going to Paisley Park. That's like Prince's Graceland."

"Oh, how FUN! Well, I won't hold you up, we just wanted to say 'hi' real quick. Do you wanna talk to Dad?"

"Sure."

"OK, here he is"

Dad got on the phone, which always blew me away because I still hadn't gotten used to the fact that my parents had got back together. They had finally divorced, remarried other people, Mom became a widow and Dad's former mistress ended up leaving him, and they ended up reconciling. At first, I wasn't a big fan of the idea, but Dad had undergone a lot of therapy for his Vietnam-related PTSD, and he was a much kinder and gentler man now, no longer prone to the terrifying fits of rage he'd put me and my siblings through as a kid. I now genuinely enjoyed talking to Dad. This wasn't the man who raised me. Thank God.

"Hey there, Dad. How are ya?"

"Good. So…Minneapolis, huh?"

"Yeah. I'm on a pilgrimage to see Prince's house. I had to do this. Can't afford it but hey, what can you do?"

"Well, have fun, son. I'll always remember seeing him in concert with you."

"Yeah, that was fun, wasn't it?"

"Sure was. Well, we'll let you go. We just wanted to say 'hi.'"

"Thanks, Dad. I love you."

"I love you too, son. Take care."

Dad hung up the phone and I felt myself smile. It felt really good to have reached a form of peace with my parents. They still went to church but they were far removed from the freaky fire and brimstone religious mania from the '80s. They had their beliefs but didn't try to force them on me or my family. I could honestly say I was cool with my parents. It had taken a lifetime to arrive there, but it was worth it.

I put the phone away and left the store, walking out to my rental car, looking around at the buildings.

Minneapolis is a really delightful city. They're damn proud of their Princely heritage. There are murals of Prince all over and near Paisley Park, there's an underpass that's been adopted as a memorial bridge. People who come to the city to pay their respects often write or draw under the bridge. I even added my own scribble to the wall: *J-Webb Was Here 3-1-19*. Cheesy, yeah, but I had to do it.

That afternoon, I met my old internet friend Kerri at a local bar. Kerri was still active on Prince.org even though the site was now quaintly outdated in the era of social media. Kerri and I used to chat a lot in the chatroom, and she always laughed at my stupid jokes. Sitting down together was a little stilted; she was one of those people who was easier to talk to online than in real life. You know how that goes. But regardless, she was very pleasant, and she paid for my drink. We parted with a friendly hug.

As evening approached, I drove to a small town called Chaska where my hotel was at, about 20 minutes outside of Chanhassen where Paisley Park stands. I checked into the hotel, which was practically vacant, and had dinner with my friend Violet at a nearby Mexican restaurant. Violet was also from the Org and we had been friends for years. She was beautiful, with red hair, green eyes, cute freckles, and a dazzling smile. There was never anything romantic between us, but it was impossible not to fall in love with her a little bit anytime I saw her. We talked about our respective jobs, about my trip so far, and she told me stories about seeing Prince all the time while she was growing up. I hung on to her every word.

After hugging Violet goodbye, I went back to my hotel and tried to sleep but it was pointless. I was too damned excited for the Paisley Park tour the next morning. After getting maybe three hours of solid sleep, I woke up around 7, got dressed, and drove to Chanhassen.

Prince told Oprah in 1996 while promoting *Emancipation* that he would always live in Minneapolis because "it's so cold it keeps all the bad people out." He wasn't kidding. Chahassen is about as isolated as you can get, a barren moon to the planet that is Minneapolis. I got to the Park two hours before my tour was scheduled, so I drove over to the nearby Caribou Coffee, where Prince used to go. Apparently, it was common to see Prince riding his bike around Chanhassen.

I told the young man behind the counter at the coffee bar that I was from Toledo and I was there to visit Paisley Park. He smiled and nodded knowingly.

"So what did Prince always used to order whenever he'd come in here?" I asked, trying to imagine how much I would trip if I had to make a coffee drink for Prince.

"A chocolate Coolata," said the young man without an ounce of hesitation. "That was his usual."

"Then in honor of the man, I'll take one of those," I said with a big smile, even though downing a frozen drink in two-degree weather didn't exactly sound pleasant. I sat at a table to keep warm, trying to imagine Prince hanging out here. Despite his superhuman talents, the man was still human.

I killed some time and then drove over to Paisley Park when it was about time for my tour. I got the VIP package because I didn't know if I would ever make it here again. If this was my only time visiting Prince's homebase, I was going to make it count. When you go in, the first thing you have to do is surrender your cell phone. No pictures, no selfies, no Instagram, no nothing. It's kind of a cool actually—you have to be fully present for the tour. No distractions.

Your tour guide greets you, and takes you into the antechamber, pointing out different rooms where Prince lived and worked. Even though there's no pictures allowed, there's a part where they take a picture of you underneath this big picture of Prince during the 3rdEyeGirl phase. Paisley Park is a delightful place to visit. You see a bunch of outfits Prince wore (and man, he really WAS tiny), the motorcycle from "Purple Rain," various studios, his big soundstage, even a little café where we were given a vegetarian sandwich and gluten-free cookie at the end of the tour.

When I was there, I did something that I simply had to do in order to achieve some kind of closure with Prince's death. I read a poem that I wrote the day after Prince died. It had been published in an anthology of poetry that was printed in the summer of 2016.

U Never Knew Me But U Were My Best Friend

U probably don't remember giving me a big hug
Christmas morning, 1991?
I got Diamonds and Pearls in my stocking
That cool hologram cover blowing my mind
Staring at it 4 hours
Listening 2 U mention Jesus
And shaking beds
N the same song
Remember Sofia?
She went by the name cherrypie319 in Prince.org
God, so long ago
Makes Facebook seem boring now
She met me N the chat room
We fell N love 2 Ur music, U know
First time we made love was 2
Disc 2 of Emancipation
Eighteen years later I still remember
That trip 2
"Erotic City"
And U were right
All the sistas do like it when U lick 'em on the knees
My daughter loves U

We listened 2 For You this morning
I bought the reissue yesterday
Is it appropriate 4 a 10-month old
2 listen 2 U talk about a love that's soft and wet?
I dunno
But do U remember when I was 18?
I had that fishing knife on my desk ready 2 open my wrist?
U sang "Anna Stesia" 2 me
And U saved me.
So U gave me love
U gave me my daughter
U gave me my life
U never knew me
But U were my best friend.

This poem summed up everything I had to say about Prince, his legacy on my life, and everything he had done for me. After I read it, there were a few sobs and sniffles from the group, and the tour guide—a great guy named Josh—told me to give the poem to the archivists in the gift shop so they could add it to the Prince collection.

With the poem in the archives, I was now an official part of Prince's legacy. It felt amazing. Finally, I was at peace with the fact that Prince was no longer on this planet. I still had his music. His movies. His lyrics. His pictures. I still had everything he had given me and millions of others on this accursed rock called Earth. We still had Prince. And we always will.

The rest of the tour was pleasant enough but my mind was elsewhere. I was reeling from being able to give something back to Prince, in some miniscule way, for how much he had given to me over the years. I wondered if Prince's ghost had heard the poem and what he thought of it. I hoped he would appreciate it and knew from what place I was coming from. That I meant it as an expression of love for all Prince had done for me over the course of my life.

There will never be anyone else like Prince and I like to think there are other young people out there right now who are being guided through their tumultuous lives with Prince serving as their spirit guide. The question "What would Prince do?" had served me well throughout most of my life and to this day, I still beg that question whenever strife hits.

I hope that Prince's legacy continues to inspire youngsters to make music and question everything they've been taught. To not be afraid to go crazy. Get nuts. To continue to look for the purple banana until they put us in the white van and take us away.

Forever.

ACKNOWLEDGEMENTS

Thank you to the following people for their inspiration, motivation, and occasional kick-in-the-ass (and in no way is this in any particular order): Kathleen Merryman, Shannon Merryman, Melissa Moshell, Becky Banas, Heather Rose, Amanda Wolfe, Mandy Hildebrand, Ryan Bunch, Hillari Snelson, Pam Weirauch, Emily Rippe-Desmond, Rachel Besterman, Nate Mattimoe, Mark and Collette Jacobs and the entire Jacobs family, Andrea Gresko, Stephanie Richardson-Hagaman, Dean Kulik, Erica Johnson, Lauren Ellis, Ann Dahl, Ben Burns (RIP), Cathy Zimmerman, Linda Wilson, Tracy Balazy, Tom Paulu, Shannon Bremer, Chris Agee, Nathan Close, Jessica Enders, Kim Ingram, Sharron Cooper, Jim Hanlen, Mike and Katy Doherty, Benti Bisson, Gary Leitzell, Erin Kanary, Pam Steck, Jordan Girton, Zeke Sadiqi, Allie Cohen, Amanda Perkins-Anderson, Walt Chancellor, Champtown, Kayla Williams, Valerie Kell (RIP), Rita Fontaine, Peter John (RIP), Megan Cruea, Elaine Anderson (RIP), Sara Meeks, Pamela Watson, Kent Houston

THE PURPLE
BANANA PEELERS

Love, appreciation, and thanks to the men and women who contributed to my GoFundMe campaign, which led to the publication of this book:

Christopher Agee

Timothy Anderl

Cap Averill

Rachel Anderson

Anonymous (2)

Rachel Besterman

Shannon Bremer

Nikki Brown

Michelle Chesko

Derek Cowan

Layne Delp

Emily Desmond

The Dude

Steve Evert

JASON WEBBER

Mandy Hildebrand
Amy Hooper
Emily Hotz
Alex Jacobs
Margot Jacobs
Erin Kanary
Phil Kaplan
Kamille Koleros
Diane Lessnau
Kelly Lopez
Mark A. Moffett
Jessica Miller
Melissa Moshell
Mary-Jo Powell
Barbara Paul
Nathan Rabin
Heather Rose
The Rivas Family
Brenna Sanchez
Jarrod Schockow
Angela Sciarabba
Jason Shaltz
Hillari Snelson
Cindy Uschan
Heidi Vossen
Alison Warfield